A Quick Guide to the Styles of I

The Anatomy of Viking Art

Jonas Lau Markussen

The Anatomy of Viking Art
A Quick Guide to the Styles of Norse Animal Ornament
Jonas Lau Markussen

© 2019 Jonas Lau Markussen
www.jonaslaumarkussen.com

This work is licensed under a Creative Commons
Attribution-NonCommercial-ShareAlike 4.0 International License.
To view a copy of this license, visit
www.creativecommons.org/licenses/by-nc-sa/4.0

2nd edition
ISBN 978-87-970600-3-2

Contents

Introduction

Norse artworks are some of the only first-hand sources concerning the people inhabiting Scandinavia in the Viking Age. But it may be very difficult and daunting to decipher the individual artworks, and even more difficult to try to recreate them, without a mental model of how the individual pieces fit together, drawn from extensive study of the works of experienced scholars. Often, the surviving original artworks are presented with little or no context, and often are also damaged or distorted due to wear and the effects of time. This guide is intended to paint a broad but cohesive picture of the styles and their development over time. It is by no means meant to be an exhaustive resource, but instead, to act as a stepping stone to help you understand the central concepts of Viking Age art.

I am neither a historian nor an archaeologist. My background is in graphic design and architecture, and this guide is intended to be the resource I wish I had when I began to try to understand the art of the Norse, and made my first unsuccessful attempts to recreate authentic artwork based on the Viking Age art styles. The guide is based on the work of knowledgeable scholars and my own studies of the archaeological artefacts. Owing to the lack of reliable documentation, and because of possible copyright concerns, all the illustrations in this guide are my own new designs, based on the principles of original Viking Age art. Creating these has been a great learning experience, and has contributed tremendously to my understanding of this art and how it is constructed.

I hope this guide will assist you in your quest to become familiar with the styles of the Norse, and get you up to speed faster than I was able to, by bypassing the otherwise challenging learning curve. I have skipped all the scholarly history and the who's who of academia in favour of getting right to the matter at hand: Viking Age art.

The thematic division of the main characteristics under the headings of shapes, outlines, flow, pattern, composition and motifs are largely based on Signe Horn Fuglesang's work, though I have made a few adjustments to fit the purposes of this guide. The art styles of the Viking Age are very much products of the times in which they developed. By including historical timelines and maps, I hope to help you better anchor the styles and their characteristics to the historical events and culture of their times, and also to make this a quick reference guide when creating artwork for re-enactment-purposes. This guide is structured chronologically, with the seven styles ordered from the earliest to the most recent, but be aware that there is still scholarly debate about the definition and categorisation of some of the styles. What I have presented here is, to my knowledge, the most plausible representation yet of the actual historical development, based on what we know so far. I encourage you to do your own research, and I have made it as easy as possible for you to look up any items referenced, or historical events mentioned in this guide.

I have published this guide under the cc-by-nc-sa license, which essentially means that as long as you copy and share the content without receiving compensation, you may do so as much as you like. So please share the knowledge with whomever you know who might find it interesting or useful.

I hope this guide will assist you in your study of Viking Age art, and also help you to recreate beautiful, authentic Norse artwork.

Enjoy!

Jonas Lau Markussen

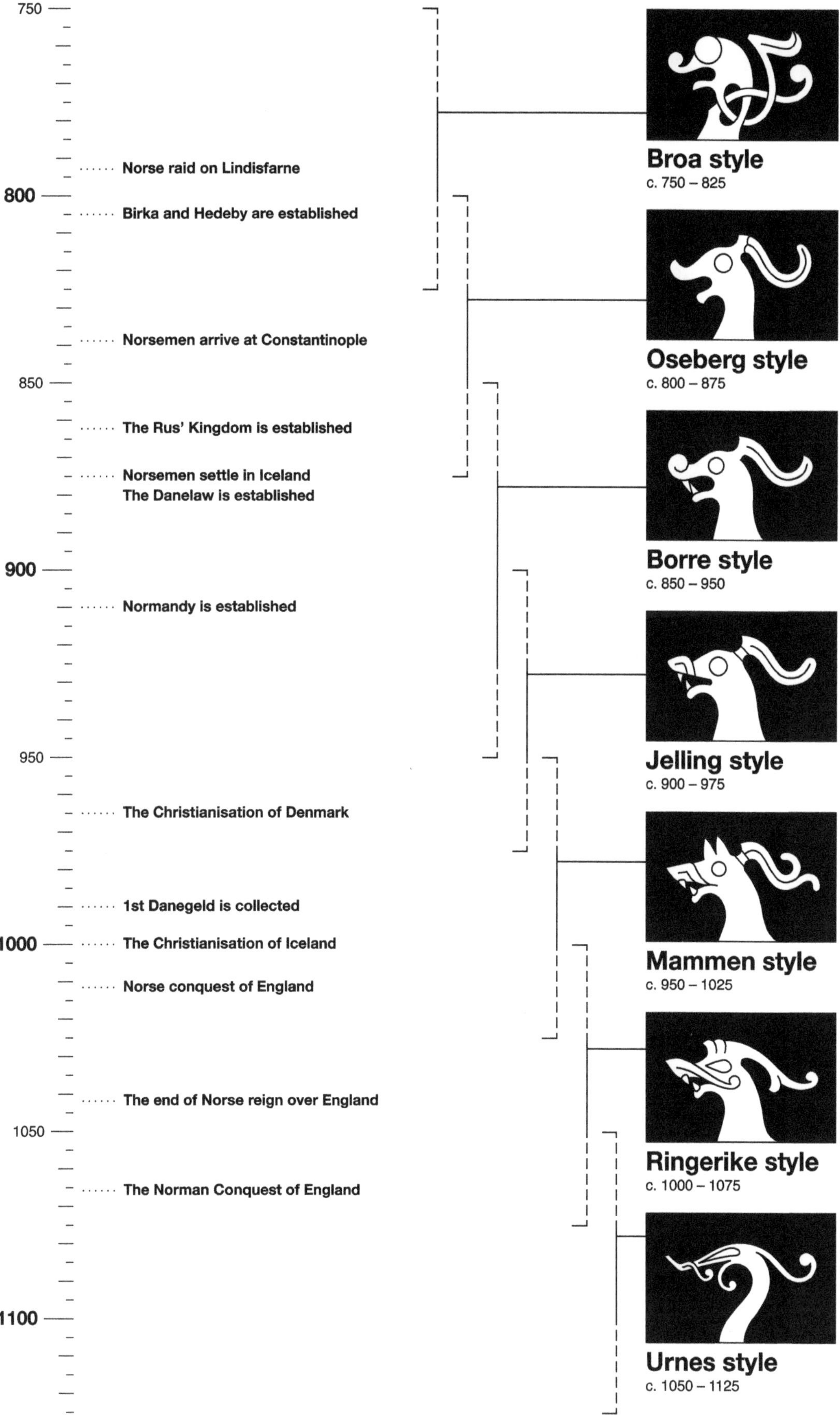
750
Norse raid on Lindisfarne
800
Birka and Hedeby are established
Norsemen arrive at Constantinople
850
The Rus' Kingdom is established
Norsemen settle in Iceland
The Danelaw is established
900
Normandy is established
950
The Christianisation of Denmark
1st Danegeld is collected
1000
The Christianisation of Iceland
Norse conquest of England
The end of Norse reign over England
1050
The Norman Conquest of England
1100
Broa style
c. 750 – 825
Oseberg style
c. 800 – 875
Borre style
c. 850 – 950
Jelling style
c. 900 – 975
Mammen style
c. 950 – 1025
Ringerike style
c. 1000 – 1075
Urnes style
c. 1050 – 1125

Broa Style

c. 750 – 825

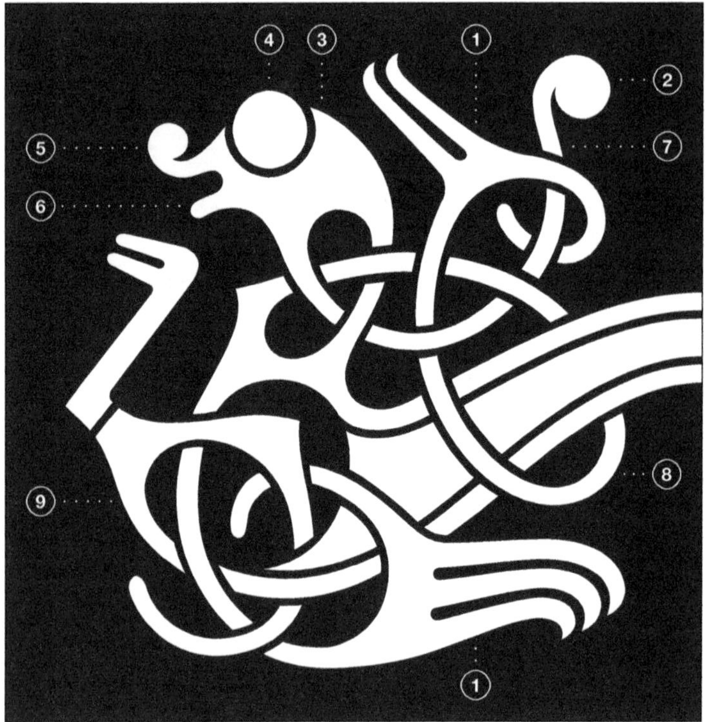

Shapes

1 Lappets with double- or triple-tendril frond terminals.
2 Tightly curled tendril terminals.
3 Head in profile.
4 Round eye.
5 Round, tightly curled snout.
6 Small and slightly curved mouth.
7 Neck tendrils.
8 Limbs rendered as extremely elongated tendrils.
9 Open hips dissolving into looping tendril interlacing.

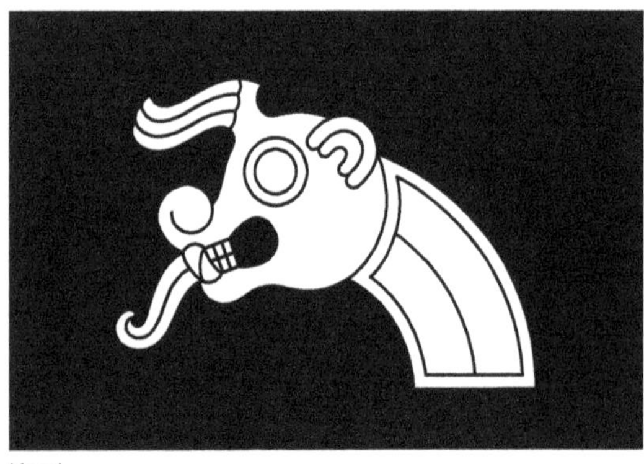

Head

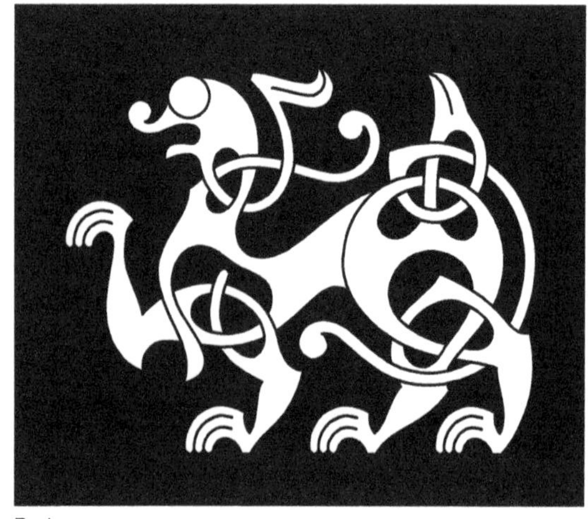

Body

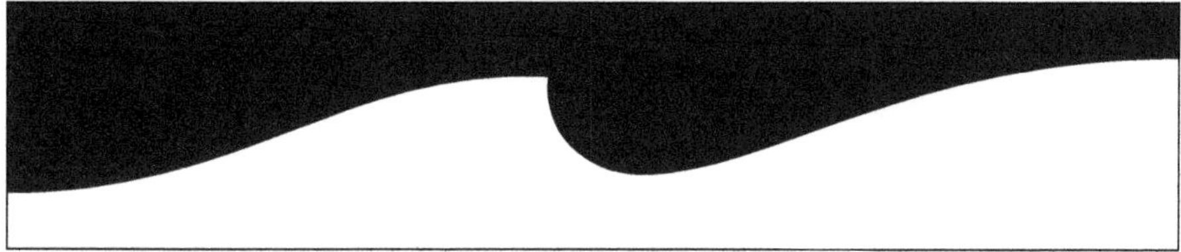

Outlines

Curved outlines with occasional kinks.

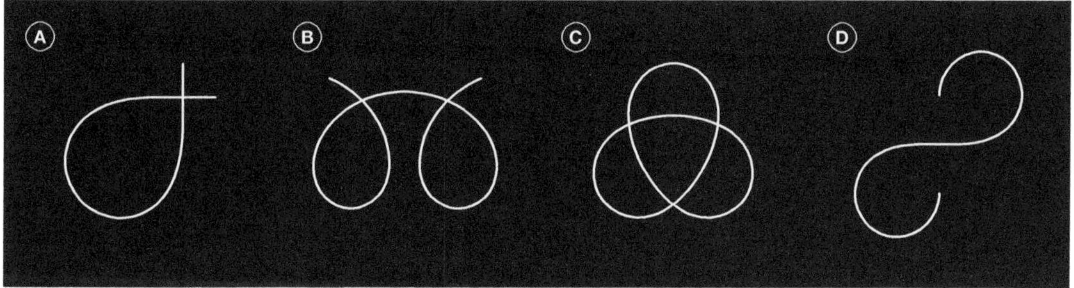

Flow

Even and almost circular curves.

A Single loops.
B Curly loops.
C Triquetra knots.
D S-shapes.

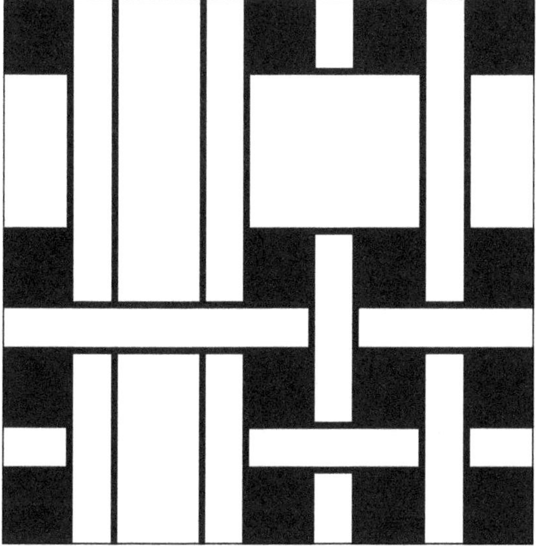

Pattern

- Semi-tight interlacing with little visible background.
- Double contour may appear.
- Single-strand ribbons.
- Double-strand ribbons may appear.

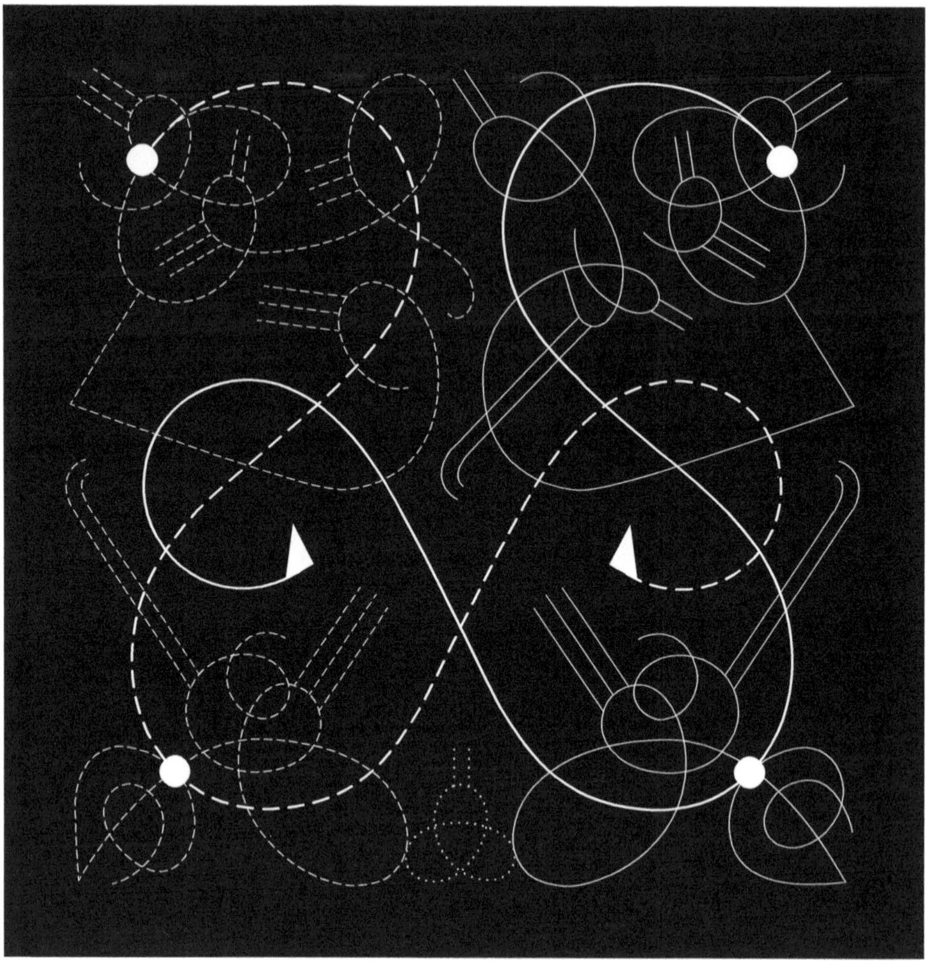

A

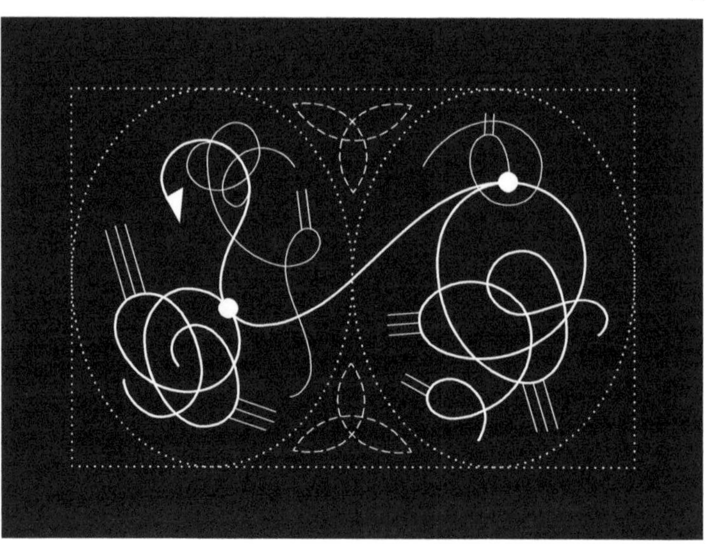

B

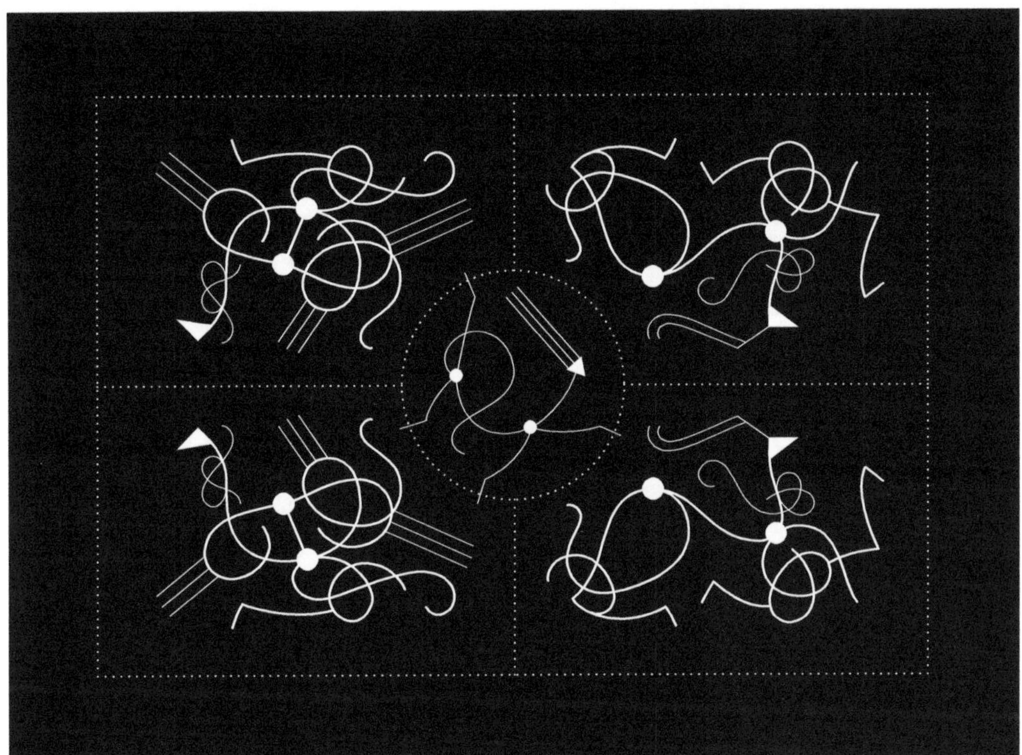

C

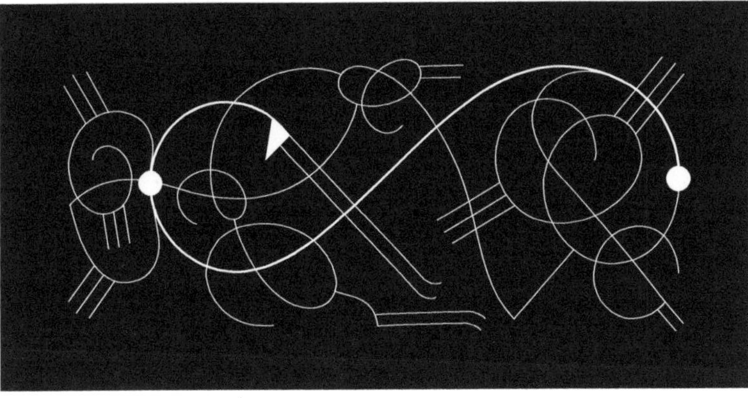

D

Composition

- Clear, almost-geometric composition.
- Repetition of basic compositional lines.
- A sense of counterpoint composition.
- Apparent symmetry in the composition – however, a difference in detail (A, C).
- Compositions often divided or separated by framework (B, C).
- Juxtaposition of different types of motifs (C).

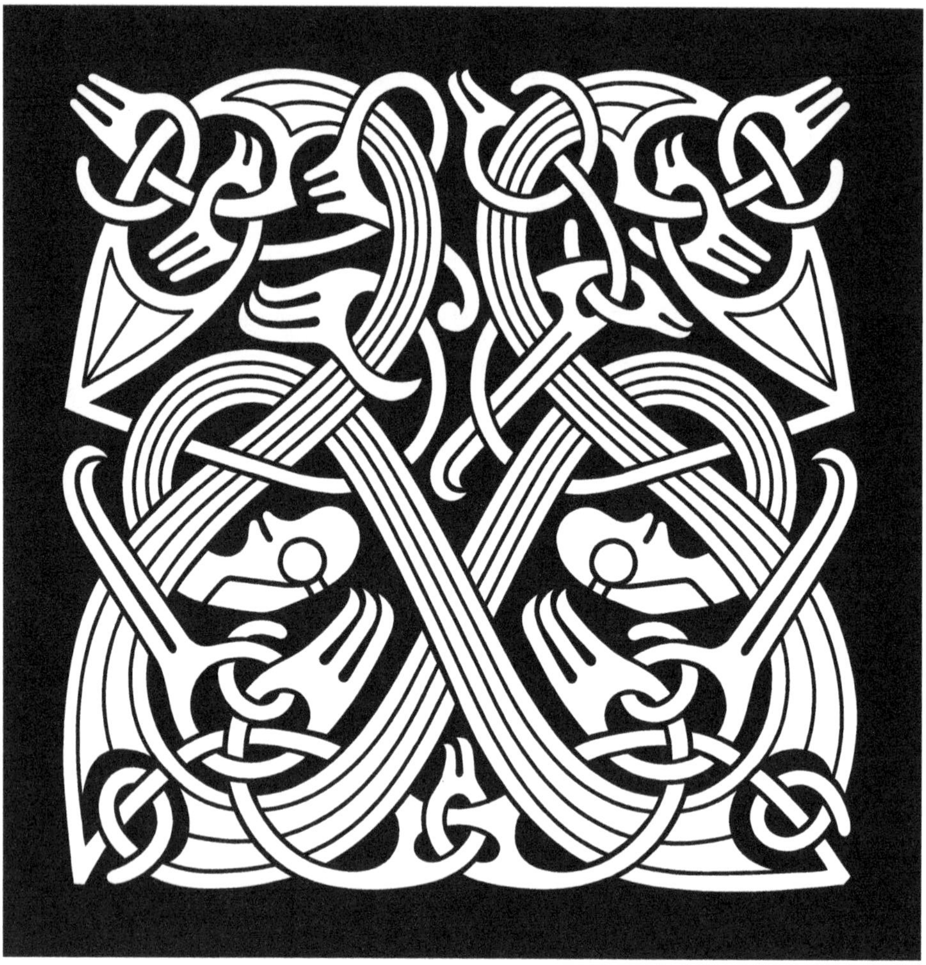

A

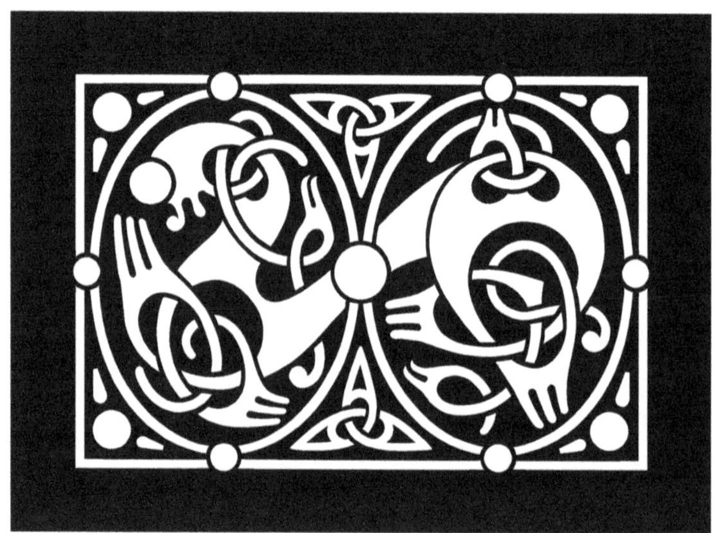

B

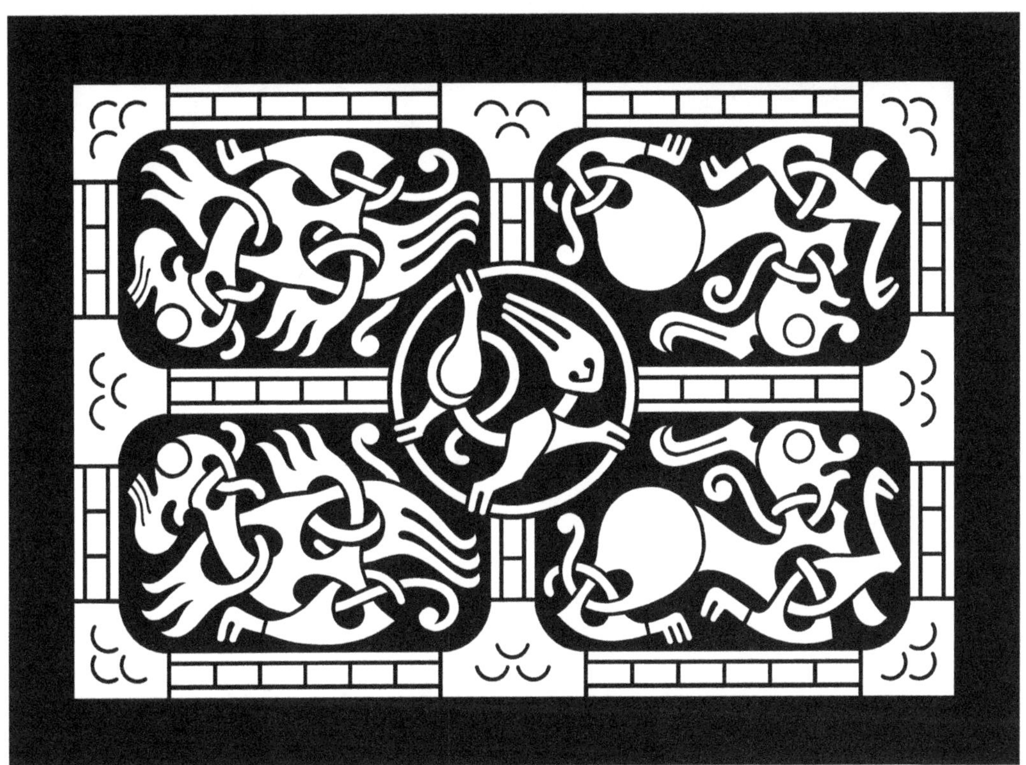

C

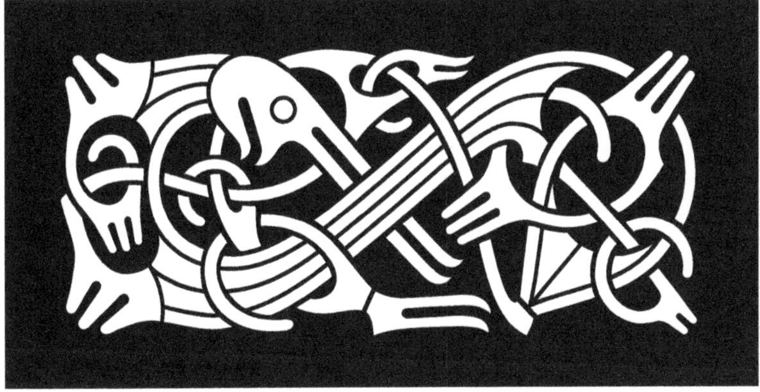

D

Motifs

- Ribbon animals with elongated bodies and extremely stylised features (A, B, D).
- Squat animals with more naturalistic bodies (B, C).
- Gripping beasts with solid bodies, ribbon-like bodies and expanded hips, and slender limbs gripping the frame or neighbouring animals or limbs (C).
- Geometric framework (B, C).

Dawn of the Viking Age

Scandinavia

Life in early Viking-age Scandinavia was centred largely around the longhouses of the farmsteads, either clustered in small villages or as single farms in the open countryside. Power structures varied, but usually a chieftain wielded the central power in local communities that comprised a number of farmsteads that swore allegiance to the chieftain. Spiritual practices were inherent to all aspects of life, and did not centre around any single religious institution such as the Christian Church. Tribute was paid to the various Norse deities, such as Odin, Freya and Thor, and whom it was of paramount importance to please with fitting sacrifices to ensure good fortune, depending on the matter at hand. The establishment of trading towns such as Hedeby and Birka typically began with temporary and seasonal marketplaces in conjunction with yearly communal *thing* assemblies that functioned as both parliaments and courts. The marketplace was typically made up of a collection of allotments along each side of the main street, with booths for commerce and makeshift workshops. These seasonal marketplaces quickly developed into more established market towns where trade could be controlled and taxes collected by the local ruler. The southern border of Scandinavia was marked by Danevirke, a fortification running across the narrowest part of the Jutland peninsula, with Hedeby at the east end, which controlled all land access to Scandinavia from the south, and connected the land trade routes with those of the sea. The gradual establishment of controlled trading towns and military structures of this magnitude indicates that some kind of ruling power, such as a king, organising and controlling subordinate chieftains and their resources, must have already been established by this time.

Europe

In the British Isles, the various Christian territories were divided into a number of kingdoms. Western Continental Europe was dominated by the expansive Frankish Empire, supported by the Catholic Church. The empire reached its peak around the year 800, when the Pope crowned Charlemagne of the Carolingian dynasty Holy Roman Emperor in Rome. Eastern Continental Europe was inhabited by a large population of Slavic clans and tribes, whose way of life and spiritual beliefs much more closely resembled those of the Norse people of Scandinavia.

Connections and Exchange

The concept of travelling and exchanging goods throughout Europe, by sea and land, was not new to the Norse, but the introduction of the sail at the beginning of the Viking Age made their already magnificent ships much faster, and therefore able to travel further. This new advantage was one of the reasons the Norse now began to be a force to be reckoned with, and they ultimately left a lasting and profound impression on European history. Though most of the journeys and exchanges of the Norse were probably relatively peaceful and based on trading goods and establishing alliances and connections, the Scandinavians are best known for their violent raids. The term 'viking' means 'pirate' in Old Norse, and was not the general name for the peoples of Scandinavia, but was used only when individuals or groups were 'going viking', that is, going pirating. In the surrounding Europe of their time, the Scandinavians were often better known as 'the Norse' or some equivalent that denoted their origins, such as 'Swedes' or 'Danes'. In the written sources, the most famous account of the Norse is the viking attack on the Monastery of Lindisfarne, on the east coast of England. This event marks what scholars traditionally regard as the beginning of the Viking Age in Scandinavia.

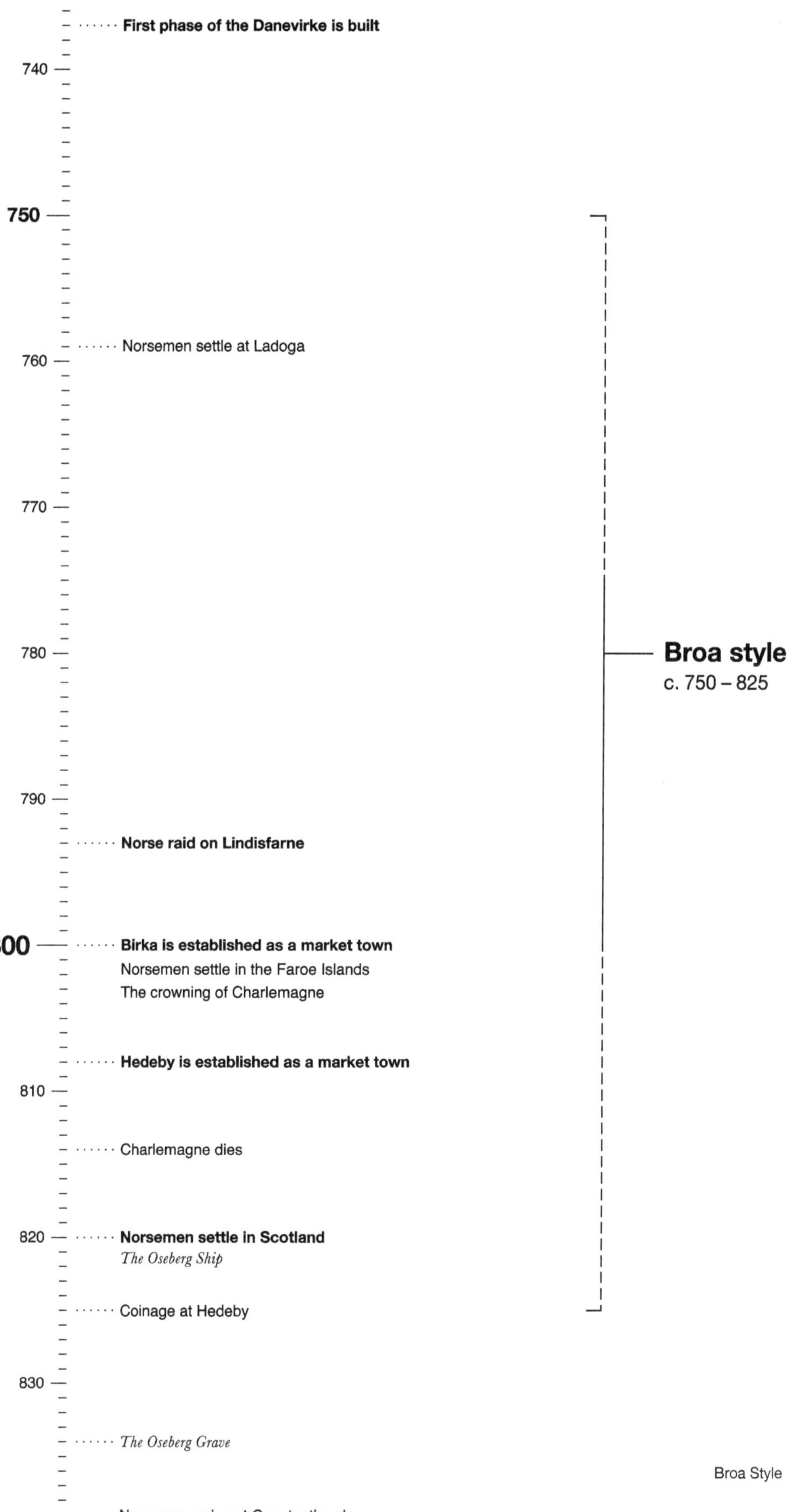
First phase of the Danevirke is built
740
750
Norsemen settle at Ladoga
760
770
780
Broa style
c. 750 – 825
790
Norse raid on Lindisfarne
800
Birka is established as a market town
Norsemen settle in the Faroe Islands
The crowning of Charlemagne
Hedeby is established as a market town
810
Charlemagne dies
820
Norsemen settle in Scotland
The Oseberg Ship
Coinage at Hedeby
830
The Oseberg Grave
Norsemen arrive at Constantinople
840
Norsemen settle in Dublin and France

Ribbon Animals & Gripping Beasts

Development

The Scandinavian artistic traditions of this time were already well-established, and several iterations of the Norse trademark, the *ribbon animal*, had been in use for a few centuries. The ribbon animals of the Broa style cover a spectrum of motifs and styles of execution. Common characteristics are heads in profile with round eyes, and open hips with intertwining, ribbon-like limbs. At one end of the spectrum, the animals are extremely abstracted, with elongated bodies, simplified facial features, and completely uniform limbs, whether they depict claws, wings or tendrils intertwined in almost geometric patterns. At the other end of the spectrum, the animals are almost naturalistic, with organic and squat bodies, while they maintain many of the characteristic features of this style. They are often pictured individually, with the only interlacing of ribbons being their own intertwining limbs. The *gripping beast*, on the other hand, does not adhere at all to conventions of ribbon animals. It is always pictured with its head facing forward, and its body is typically curled up in a single pretzel-knot-like interlacing, with solid hips. Its feet always grasp either itself or the surrounding frame of the ornament. The individual motifs themselves, whether ribbon animals or gripping beasts, are almost always surrounded by, or interlace with, a geometric framework, typically ovals or squares that hold together the composition. The British Isles were an artistic centre at this time, but the Norse also felt the influence of the Anglo-Carolingian art of the Frankish regions. In particular, the semi-organic animals and birds must have derived from European art in some way, as they do not seem to have any predecessors in Scandinavian tradition, though they were developed dramatically to fit it, and it is almost impossible to trace them back to their European sources of inspiration. The motif of the gripping beast that emerges in the Broa style may also have been somehow inspired by these external sources, but at the same time, it is a distinctly Norse motif, developed within the Scandinavian tradition, with no direct precursors outside of Scandinavia.

Dating

Dating early Viking Age art styles is difficult, and rests partly on the typology of objects and partly on related, dateable Anglo-Carolingian ornaments, which means that any distinctions should be viewed with caution.

The Broa Mounts

The Broa style is popularly named for the horse-harness mounts found in Broa, Sweden, but is formally known as Style III/E or just Style E. The Broa mounts display a comprehensive collection of almost all imaginable compositions and motifs of this style, with the occasional gripping beast added to the mix, and include some motifs not found elsewhere, such as the animal-head pieces and almost-human-like terminals on some of the mounts.

Disc-on-bow Brooches

The various disc-on-bow brooches typically display the more abstracted and elongated versions of the ribbon animals of this style, juxtaposed with segments of gripping beast motifs.

The Oseberg Academician's Work

The so-called Academician's work from the Oseberg grave displays some fine examples of wood carving in this style, though they may be on the cusp of transitioning into the subsequent Oseberg style.

Distribution

The Broa style is found only in Scandinavia, and is especially common in eastern Scandinavia.

Examples

Dateable

c. 834
The Animal-head post / The Lion Head – the Oseberg Grave
Oseberg, Vestfold, Norway.
Universitetets Oldsakssamling, Oslo C55000 172

c. 834
The Academician's Animal-head Post – the Oseberg Grave
Oseberg, Vestfold, Norway.
Universitetets Oldsakssamling, Oslo C55000 100

c. 834
The Academician's Sledge Pole from Gustafson's Sledge – the Oseberg Grave
Oseberg, Vestfold, Norway.
Universitetets Oldsakssamling, Oslo C55000 179

Undateable

Animal-shaped mount
Lamøya, Kaupang, Tjølling, Vestfold, Norge.
Universitetets Oldsakssamling, Oslo C27220n

The Broa Mounts
Broa, Gotland, Sweden.
Historiska Museet, Stockholm SHM 10796:1, SHM 11106:1

Disc-on-bow brooches
Gumbalda, Gotland, Sweden.
Historiska Museet, Stockholm SHM 1078, SHM 1361

Disc-on-bow brooch (I)
Broa, Halla, Gotland, Sweden.
Historiska Museet, Stockholm SHM 19734

Disc-on-bow brooch (II)
Melhus, Overhalla, Nordtrøndelag, Norway.
T 6574

Disc-on-bow brooch (III)
Othemars, Othem, Gotland, Sweden.
Historiska Museet, Stockholm SHM 4555

Disc-on-bow brooch (IV)
Storhaugen, Stavanger, Rogaland, Norway.
B 488

Openwork mount
Othem, Gotland, Sweden.
Historiska Museet, Stockholm SHM 11887

Oval brooch (I)
Gesala, Romafortuna, Västmanland, Sweden.
Historiska Museet, Stockholm SHM 31030

Oval brooch (II)
Södra Alby, Hulterstad, Oland, Sweden.
Historiska Museet, Stockholm SHM 7584

Round 'box-shaped' brooch (I)
Valla, Gotland, Sweden.
Historiska Museet, Stockholm

Round 'box-shaped' brooch (II)
Klause, Klinte sn., Gotland, Sweden.
Historiska Museet, Stockholm GF C 8099

Round 'box-shaped' brooch (III)
Gotland, Sweden.
Historiska Museet, Stockholm GF C 3506

Sword hilt
Steinsvik, Norway.
Universitetets Oldsakssamling, Oslo C20317a

Sword pommel
Stora Ihre, Hellvi, Gotland, Sweden.
Historiska Museet, Stockholm SHM 20550

Oseberg Style

c. 800 — 875

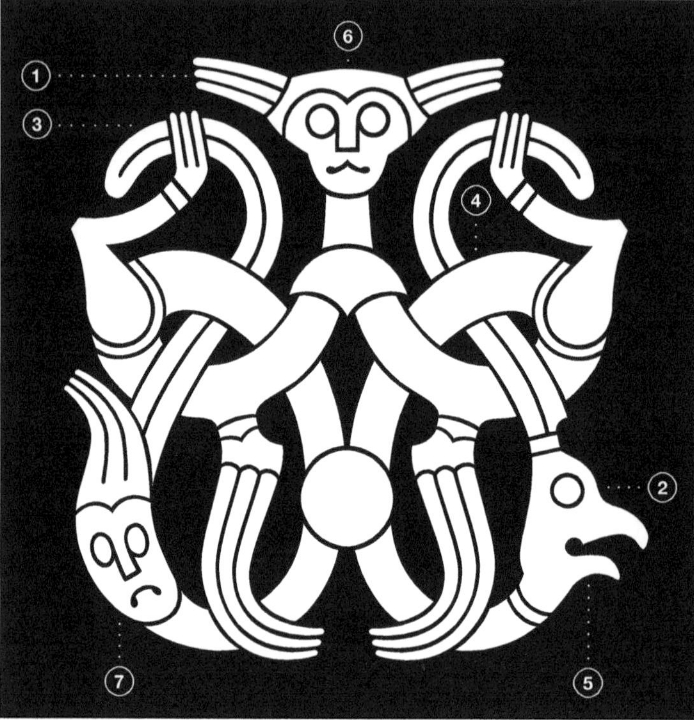

Shapes

Equally-sized squat animals:

1 Frond-like terminals.

2 Round eyes.

3 Feet grip surrounds.

An interplay of geometric and zoomorphic patterns:

4 Limbs segmented into ornamental elements.

Three main animal types:

5 Birds:

- Head in profile.
- Beaked.

6 Mask A:

- Head facing forward.
- Fronds protruding from either side of the head.

7 Mask B:

- Head facing forward.
- Top of head terminates in fronds.

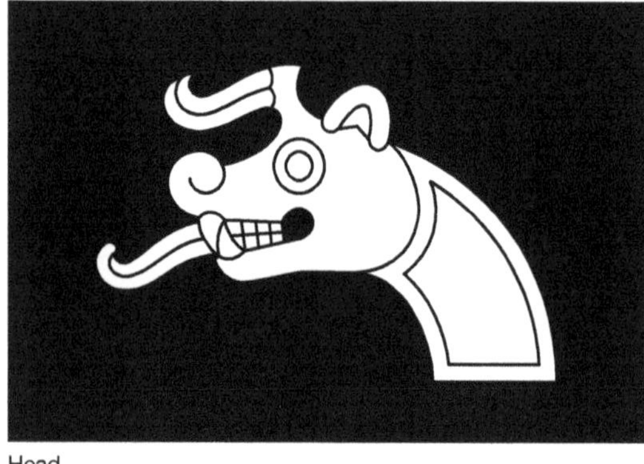

Head

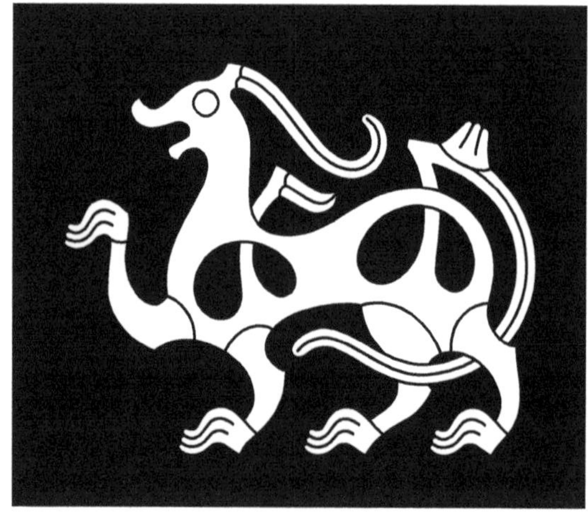

Body

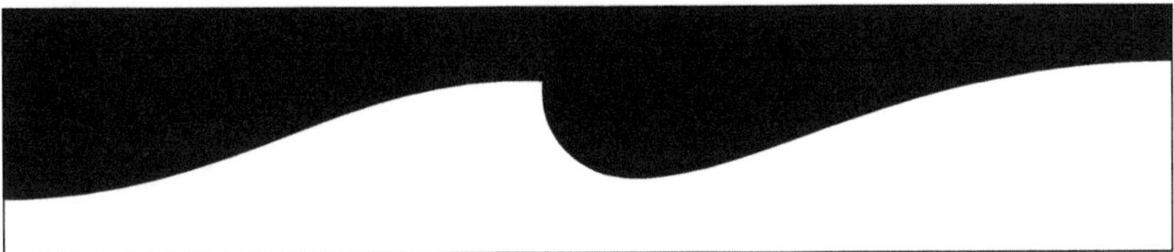

Outlines

Curved outlines with occasional kinks.

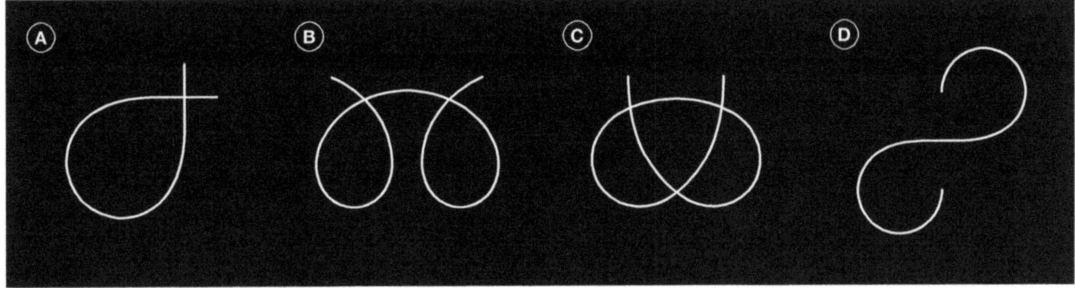

Flow

A medley of looping and waving curves.

A Single loops.
B Curly loops.
C Pretzel knots.
D S-shapes.

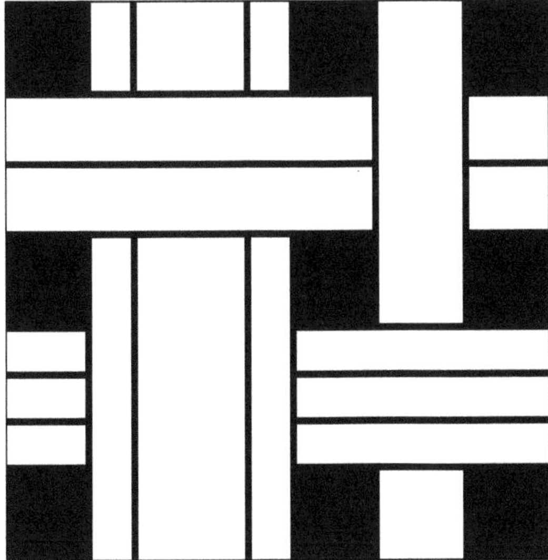

Pattern

- Tight interlacing with almost no visible background.
- Double contour.
- Single-strand ribbons.
- Double-strand ribbons.
- Triple-strand ribbons.
- A mix of high and low relief.

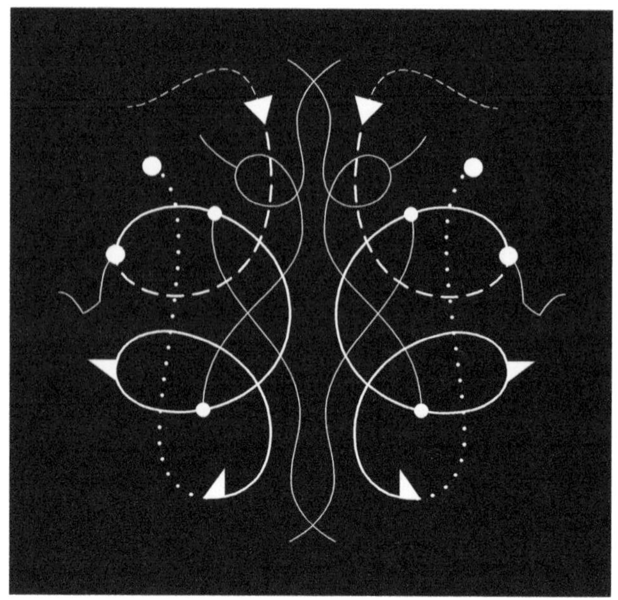

A

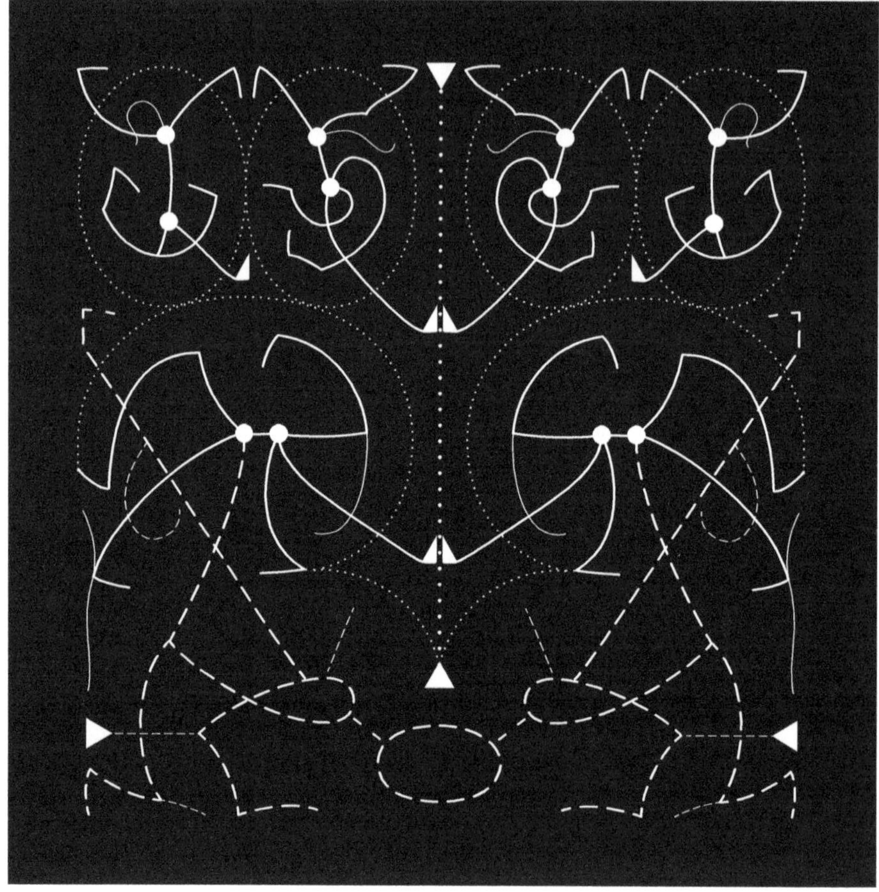

B

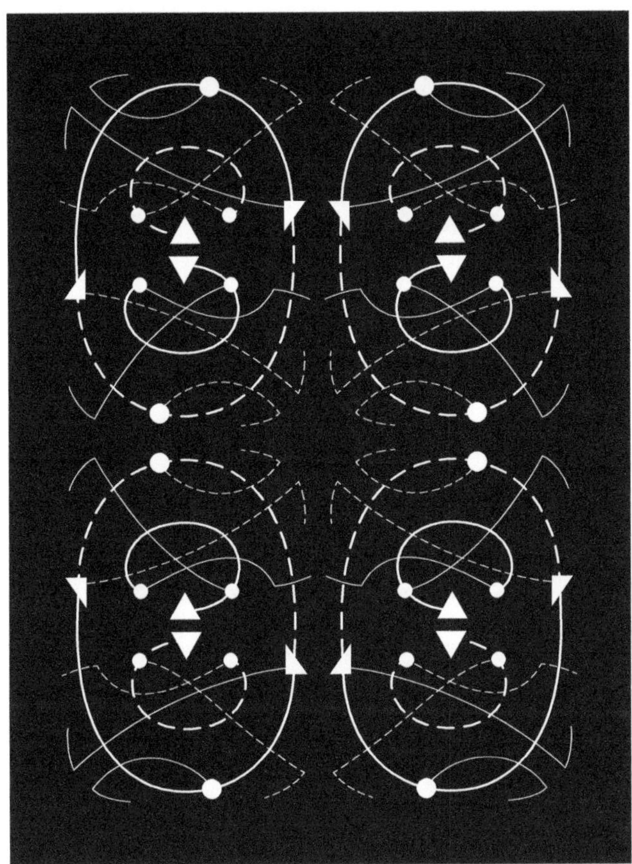

C

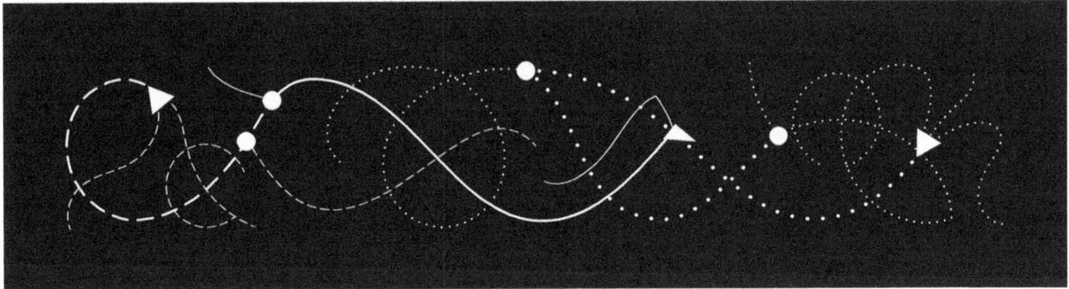

D

Composition

- An absence of main compositional lines (A, D).
- Carpet-like distribution of motifs of equal size and equal compositional value.
- Geometric and zoomorphic framework, oval or rhomboid (B, C).
- Apparent symmetry in the composition; however, differences in detail (A, B, C).

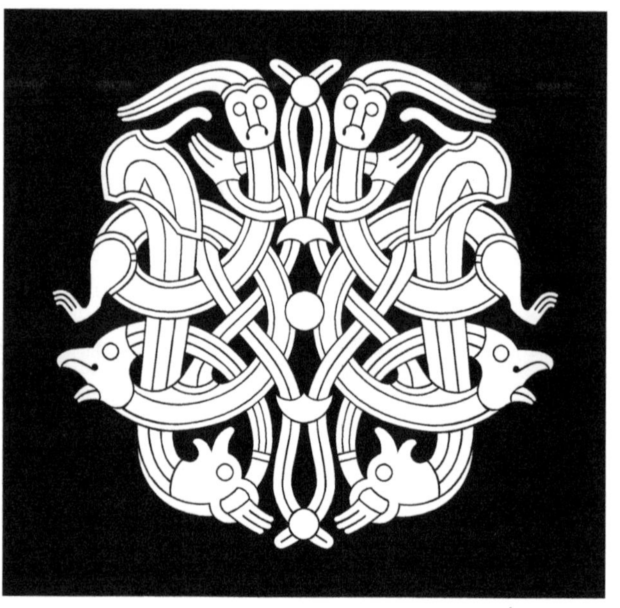

A

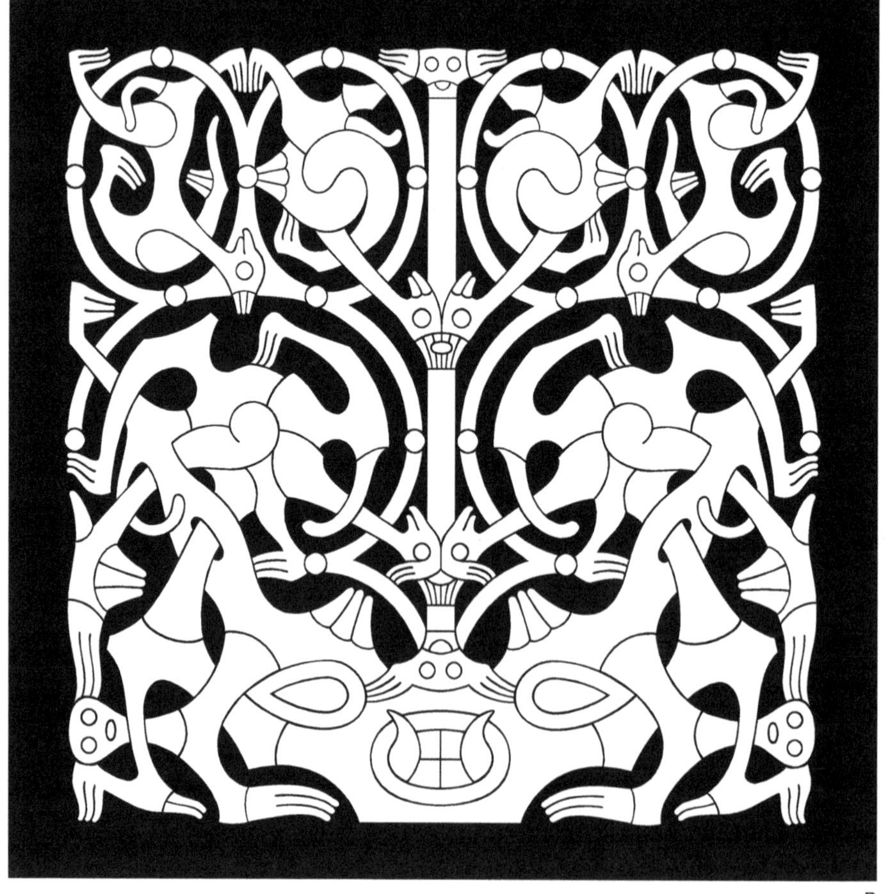

B

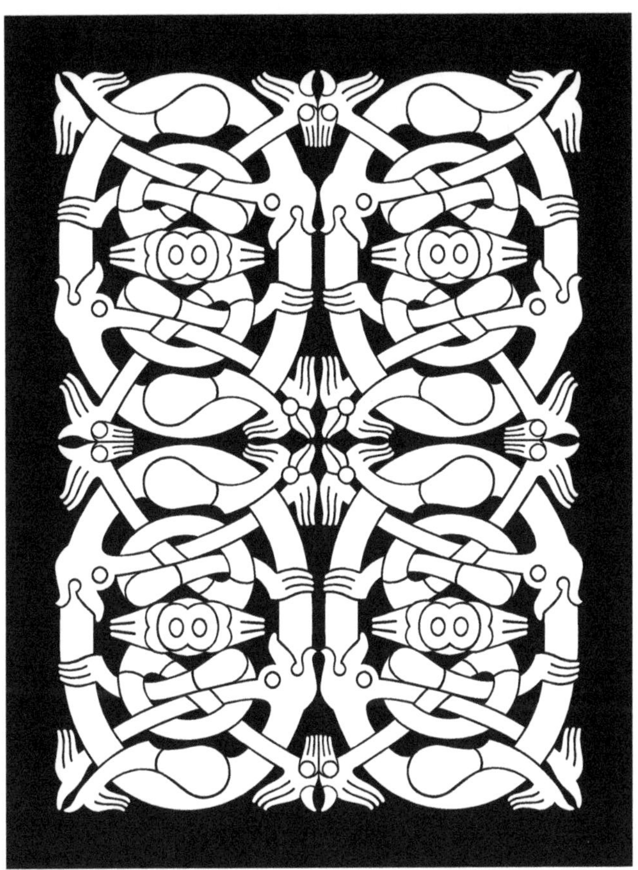

C

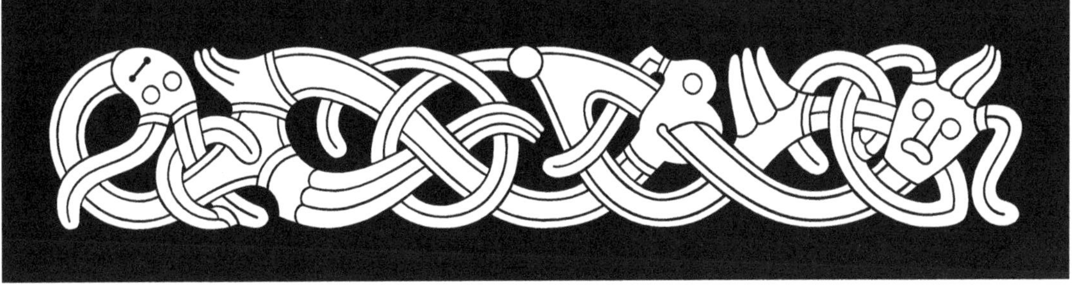

D

Motifs

- An eclectic medley of animal bodies rendered as interconnecting segments.
- Zoomorphic framework (C).
- Geometric framework (B).

Exchange and Early Expansion

Trade and Raids

The spirit of the Norse expeditions and their exchanges with the communities of the surrounding European regions was mostly opportunistic. Whether these were for trade, raid or settlement depended on the individual circumstances. Several Norse trading towns were well-established along the popular trading routes. They were centres of fluctuating cosmopolitan influences and material goods, and manifestations of all the connections with the various European tribes and societies through the far-reaching trading routes, overseas and along the continental rivers. These towns soon became powerful cultural hubs at several levels: economic, military, social, religious and artistic. Therefore, for the local rulers that collected taxes and controlled who and what entered and left the territory, control over these places was crucial.

The Eastern Routes

The Swedish trading town of Birka was the gateway to Eastern Europe. From here, all the Slavic regions could be reached by the rivers from the Baltic Sea, such as the Volga and Dnieper, eventually reaching Constantinople, the capital of the Byzantine Empire. The Norse, or the Rus' as they were known in Eastern Europe, came from what is today Roslagen, the coastal areas of Uppland in modern-day Sweden, and settled along the northern parts of these routes, to make the journeys more convenient and to be better able to trade with and raid the local Slavic tribes. The Rus' chieftain, Rurik, gained control of the Ladoga trading post, and later established a settlement further south, at Novgorod.

The Western Routes

Hedeby, situated at the southern border of Scandinavia, was the gateway to Western and Central Continental Europe. Bordering the mighty Catholic Frankish Empire to the south, and connected with the British Isles to the west through the Baltic Sea, and the rest of Scandinavia to the east through the North Sea, Hedeby was a crossroads for religious, monetary and cultural influences. Continual traffic in material goods flowed through the town. The Orkney, Shetland and Faroe Islands were settled by Norse emigrants who saw an opportunity in moving their households to these almost uninhabited and fertile islands, and making a new life. The islands soon became a bridgehead for further expeditions to, and raids on Scotland and the rest of the British Isles. The Frankish emperor, Louis the Pius, appointed Bishop Ansgar as missionary to the northern lands, and in turn, the Norse rulers allowed him to build churches in some of the most important trading towns. But as the Frankish Empire crumbled, the power, need or incentive to force the Christian faith on the 'barbarians' of the North lacked the support it needed to be successful, and as most of the Norse people saw no reason to convert, the first attempts at Christianising the North were largely futile.

790

Norsemen raid Lindisfarne

800 **Birka is established as a market town**
Norsemen settle in the Faroe Islands
The crowning of Charlemagne

Hedeby is established as a market town

810

Charlemagne dies

820 **Norsemen settle in Scotland**
The Oseberg Ship

Coinage at Hedeby

830

Oseberg style
c. 800 – 875

The Oseberg Grave

Norsemen arrive at Constantinople

840

Norsemen settle in Dublin and France

First churches are built in Scandinavia

850 **Norsemen settle by the Thames near London, England**
The Hon Hoard

Norsemen raid in Spain, North Africa, Rhône Valley and Italy

860

The Rus' Kingdom is established by Oleg

The Great Heathen Army invades England

870 **Harald Fairhair unites Norway**

Norsemen settle in Iceland

The Danelaw is established

880

890

A Remix of Conventions

Development

It is difficult to pinpoint and document what the style between the Broa and Borre styles may have looked like, and various theories have been proposed. This guide presents a type of style primarily represented by the Oseberg ship-grave, which has been dendrochronologically dated to a period between the Broa and the Borre styles. The Oseberg burial mound features some magnificent woodwork, comprising sledges, wagons, a ship, tent poles and more. Among the artefacts are some artworks done in an unmistakably Broa style. In conjunction with this, there are also many works that do not seem to fit the Broa style proper. Although they seem to feature many of the same characteristics, they also consistently and radically differ in many distinct ways. It seems that these works may represent a development of the Broa style in a new direction, which in some ways suggests the Borre style. For instance, the ribbon-like animals clearly refer back to the elegant and abstract ribbon animals of the Broa style, whereas the emphasis on the squatter shapes of the animals and the way they now consistently grasp each other and the surrounding frames suggest the application of the gripping beast of the Borre style. Even the mix of heads in profile, typical of the Broa style, and forward-facing heads, typical of the Borre style, suggests that this style represents a possible transition between the two styles. The Oseberg style is a clear development of the Norse traditions, and has no traceable influences from outside of Scandinavia. The style generally features a more relaxed and unconventional take on animal ornament. Traditionally, the individual animal of the ornament interlacing would always be depicted as a clear but extremely abstracted representation of a single, somewhat anatomically correct animal, typically with one head, one body, two or four legs and a tail. However, in the Oseberg style there is often no distinction among the individual animals in the ornament. Animal limbs and bodies are all thrown together in an eclectic mix to create the liveliest multi-level intertwining ornaments possible. Even the Broa style conventions of clearly distinguishing among, and separating the ribbon animals and the gripping beasts seem completely disregarded, as the features of each are typically merged together.

The Sledge Poles

The two sledge poles display a geometric framework similar to the Broa style, but the execution of the animals departs from it. They are mostly single and whole animals, but they occasionally blend together to fit the structure of the ornamental lines and framework.

The Baroque Animal-head Posts

On the two Baroque animal-head posts, the seemingly geometric framework is actually created entirely of the animals' limbs, disregarding the individual animals completely, and separating their body parts into mere ornamental segments to produce a composition abundant in ornate elements.

The Fourth Sledge and Gustafson's Sledge

On Gustafson's Sledge and the Fourth Sledge, we see the mixed and merged animal ornament in a more free-flowing composition of elements, without any apparent intention of imitating a geometric framework.

Distribution

The Oseberg style, like the Broa style, is unknown outside of Scandinavia, which suggests that the style had developed into the succeeding Borre style before the expansion of the Norse world into more permanent settlements in regions outside of Scandinavia.

Examples

Dateable

c. 834
Animal-head posts
– the Oseberg Grave
Oseberg, Vestfold, Norway.
Universitetets Oldsakssamling, Oslo O 1904:345, O 1904:344

c. 820
The ship
– the Oseberg Grave
Oseberg, Vestfold, Norway.
Universitetets Oldsakssamling, Oslo C550001

c. 834
The Baroque Animal-head Post
– the Oseberg Grave
Oseberg, Vestfold, Norway.
Universitetets Oldsakssamling, Oslo C55000 123

c. 834
The Baroque Sledge Poles
– the Oseberg Grave
Oseberg, Vestfold, Norway.
Universitetets Oldsakssamling, Oslo C55000 196, C55000 17

c. 834
The Carolingian Animal-head Post
– the Oseberg Grave
Oseberg, Vestfold, Norway.
Universitetets Oldsakssamling, Oslo C55000 173

c. 834
The Fourth Sledge
– the Oseberg Grave
Oseberg, Vestfold, Norway.
Universitetets Oldsakssamling, Oslo C55000 208

c. 834
Shetelig's Sledge
– the Oseberg Grave
Oseberg, Vestfold, Norway.
Universitetets Oldsakssamling, Oslo C55000 195

c. 850
Gilt silver pendants
– the Hon Hoard
Hon, Buskerud, Norway.
Universitetets Oldsakssamling, Oslo C747 (The hoard: C719-51)

Undateable

Sword sheath ferrule
Korosten, obl. Žitomir, Ukraine.
Gosudarstvennyj Istoričeskij Muzej, Moscow 105009,inv. 2575/1

Borre Style

c. 850 — 950

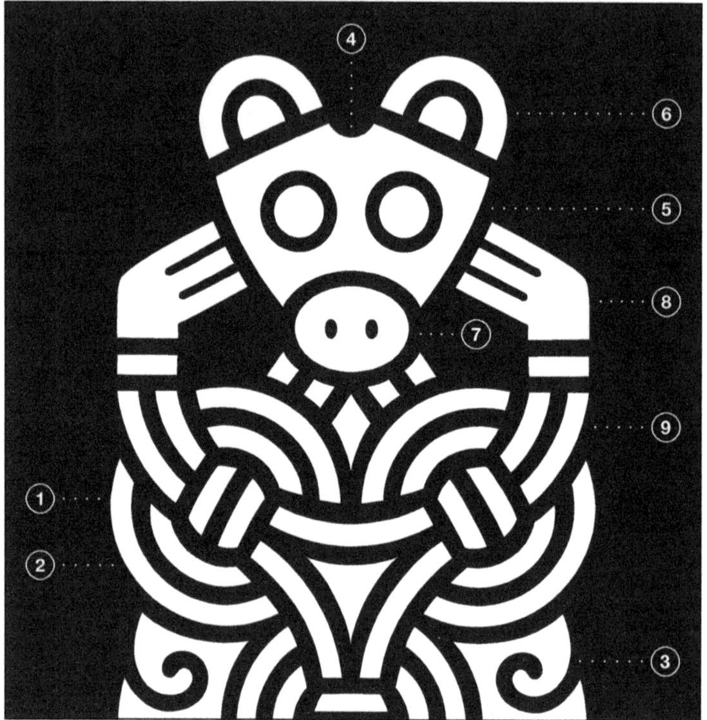

Shapes

1 Tight, knot-like interlacing.
2 Equal-sided geometric figures (circles and squares).
3 Spirals.
4 Triangular head facing forward.
5 Round or almond-shaped eyes.
6 Protruding ears.
7 Oval snout.
8 Short and squat proportions.
9 Slim and elongated legs.

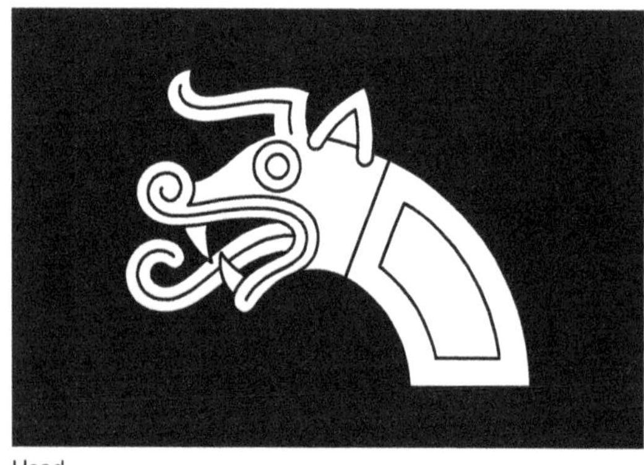

Head

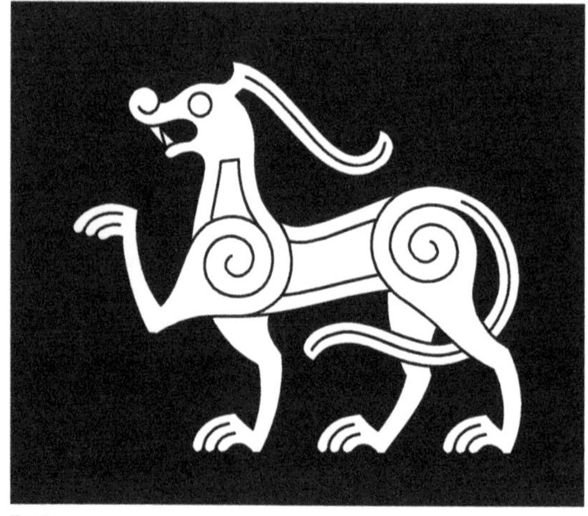

Body

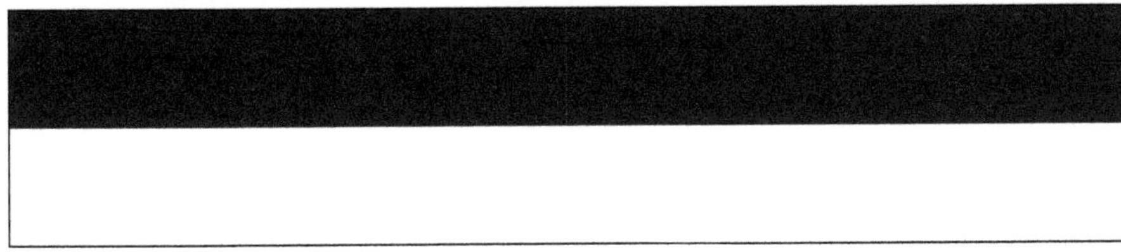

Outlines

Even outlines without tapering or indents.

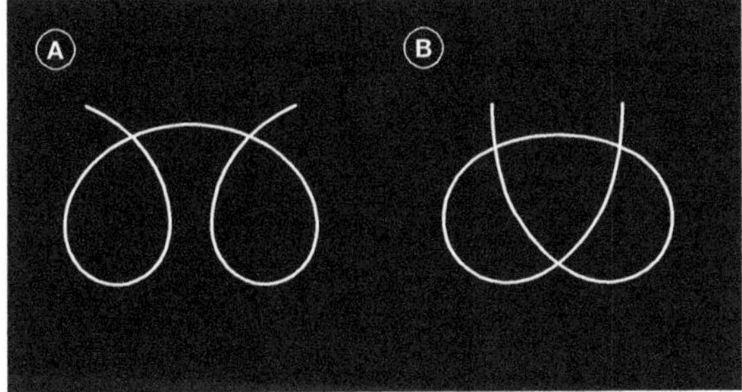

Flow

Circular curves favoured.

A Curly loops.
B Pretzel knots.

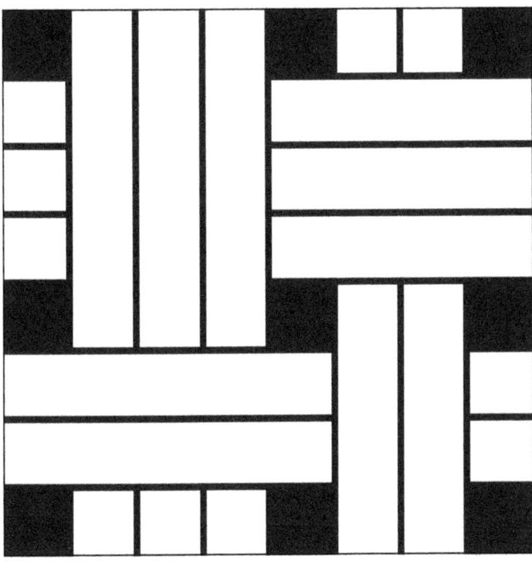

Pattern

- Very tight interlacing with almost no visible background.
- Double contours may appear.
- Double-strand ribbons.
- Triple-strand ribbons.
- High relief.

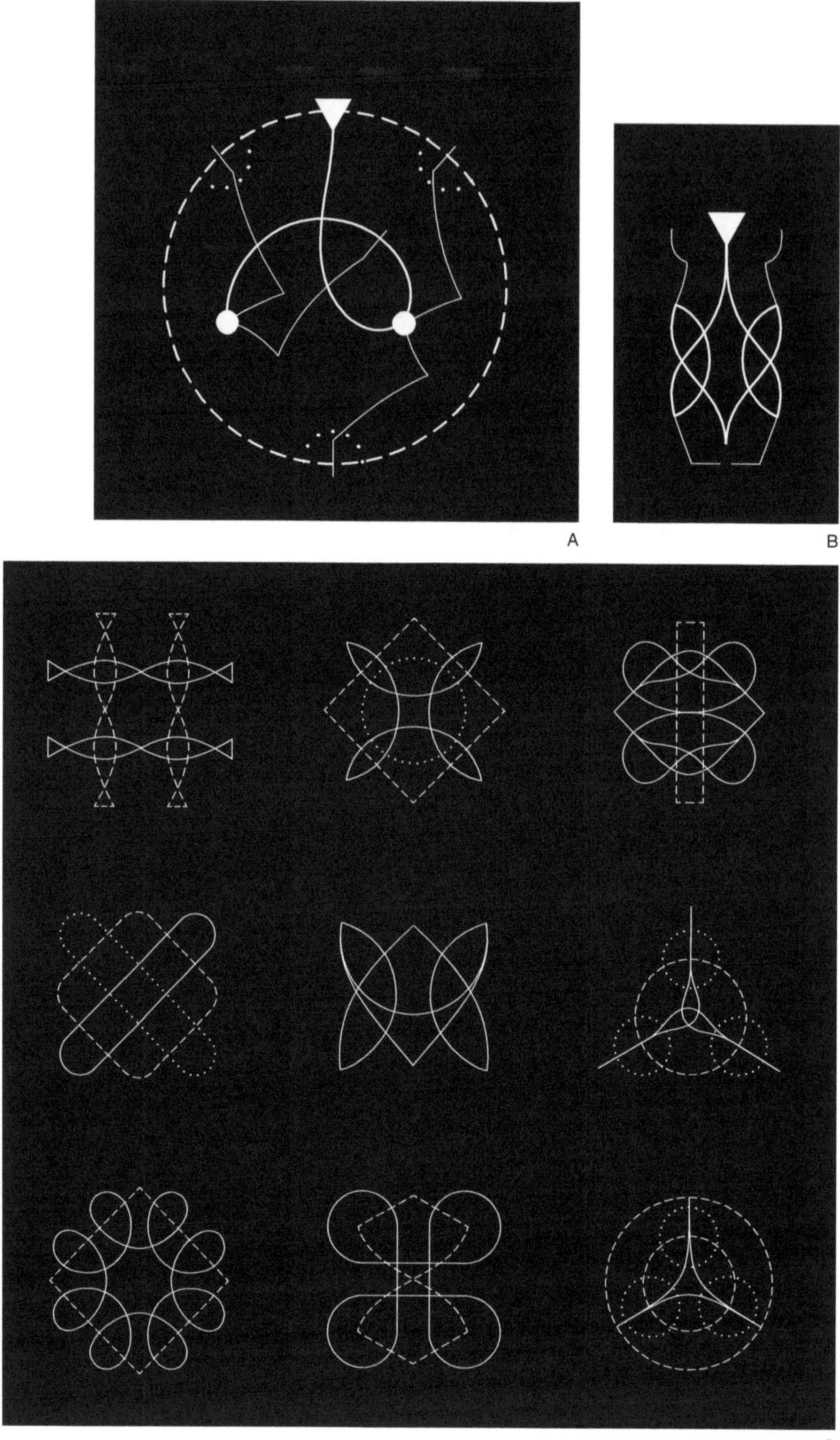
A
B
C

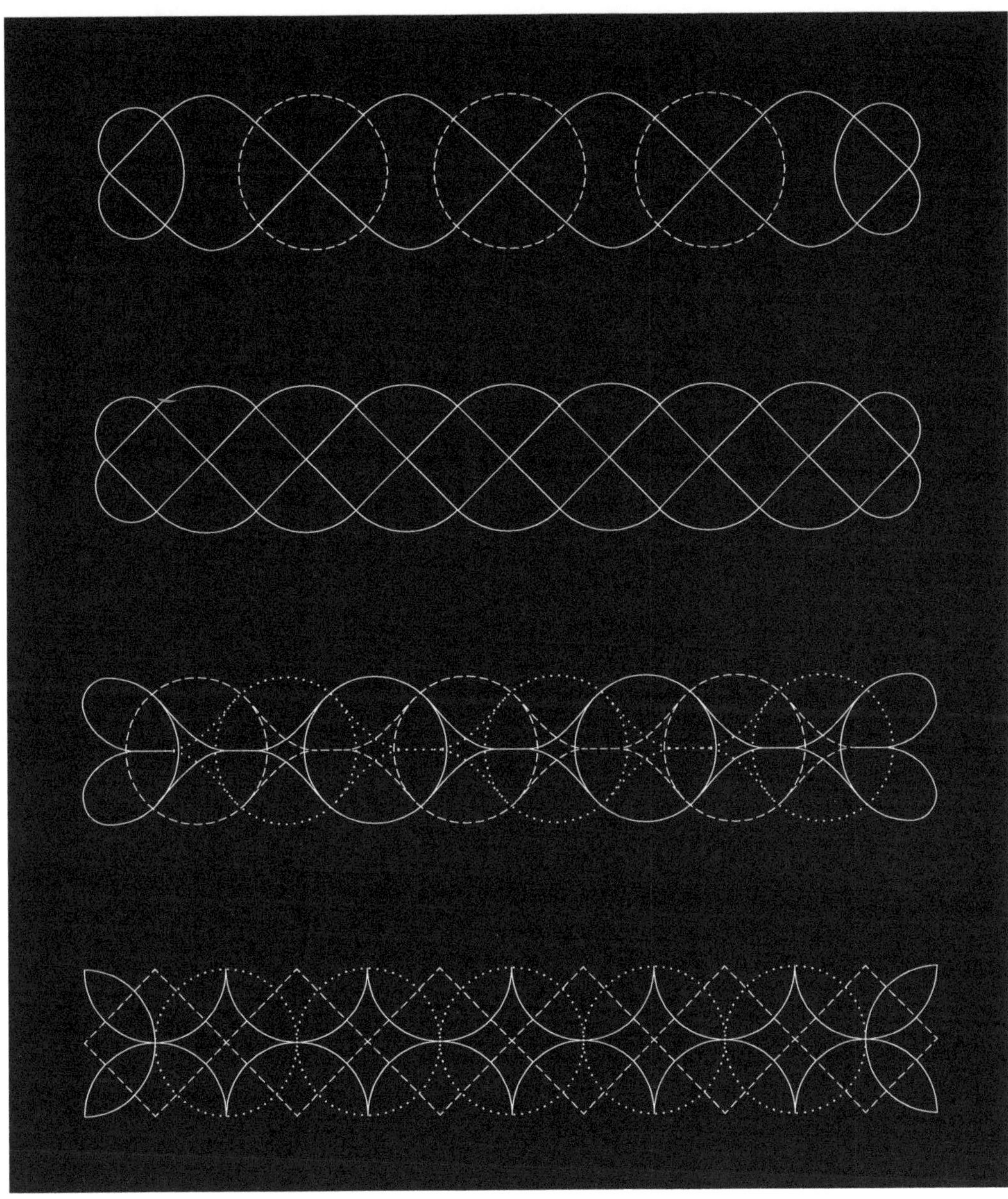
D

Composition

- Tight compositions of closed ribbons (D), knots (B, C) and animals (A, B).
- Repetition and juxtaposition of geometric shapes (C, D).

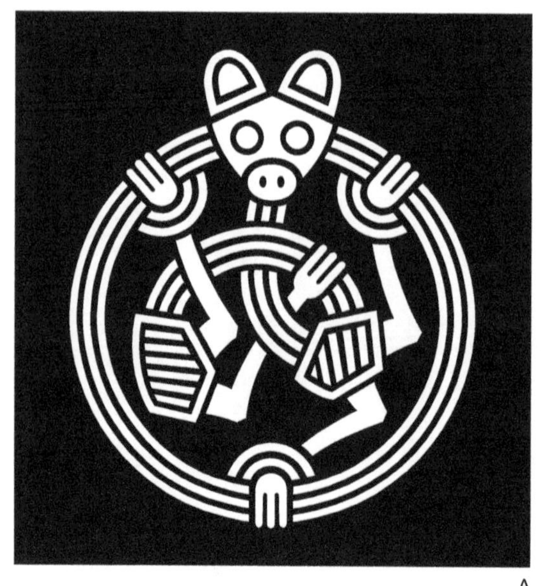

A

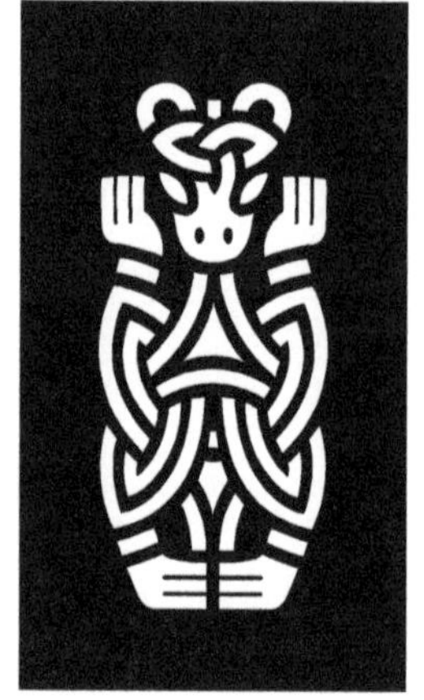

B

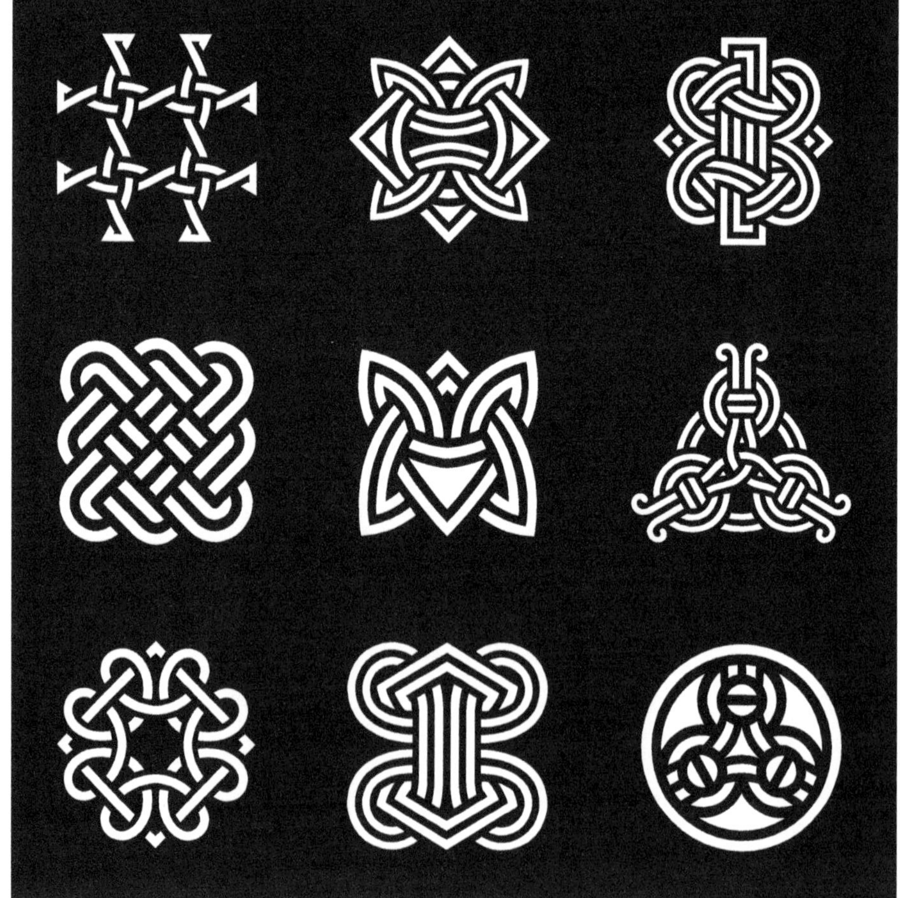

C

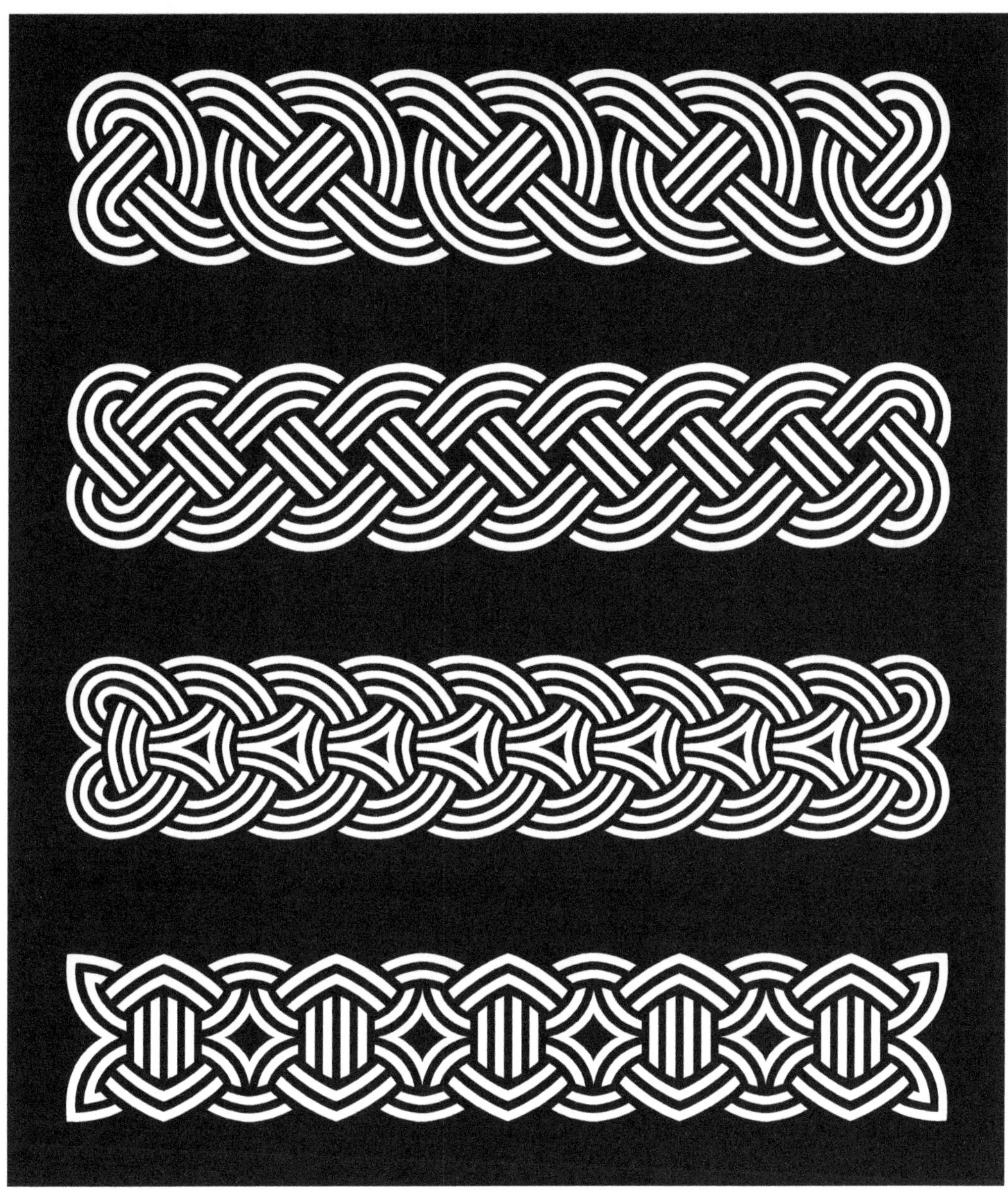

D

Motifs

- Gripping beasts (A, B).
- Ring chains composed of repeating and juxtaposed equilateral geometric shapes of closed interlacing ribbons (D).
- Single knots built by interlacing closed ribbons in geometric shapes or pretzel knot patterns (B, C).

Conquest and Colonisation

Unification of Norway

The Norwegian chieftain, Harald Fairhair, united Norway after his victory in the Battle of Hafrsfjord, and became the first King of Norway. Many of the subjugated petty Norwegian chieftains were dissatisfied with his rule and his taxation of their land, and in their pursuit of freedom, they migrated to other Norse territories.

The Icelandic Commonwealth

The newly discovered island of Iceland was a particularly popular place for the Norwegian emigrants to settle, as there was plenty of fertile land to claim, and soon all the land was acquired by Norse families. To regulate the Icelandic Commonwealth and settle disputes between feuding clans, a legislative and judicial assembly, the All-thing, was formed.

The Danelaw

The coastline of the British Isles had already been raided numerous times when the so-called Great Heathen Army invaded the English Kingdoms. Through a number of military campaigns, allegedly led by Ivar the Boneless, the Norse army was able to first capture the city of York, and then all Northumbria, then Nottingham and Mercia, followed by London and East Anglia. When they encountered the resistance of King Alfred of Wessex, the Norse, now led by Guthrum the Old, had to surrender and sign the treaty that established the boundaries of the Norse territory on the British Isles, known as the Danelaw. Many of the Norse settled permanently in the Danelaw, and in time they became integrated with the original local communities. Norse groups even invaded the territory around Dublin, and established the Norse Kingdom of Dublin.

Normandy

Norse groups continuously raided the coasts of what is today western France, where the treasures at monasteries were guarded only by monks, who were easy prey. The Norse eventually travelled up the Seine, reaching Paris, spreading terror on their way. To put an end to the Norse assaults, the French King Charles the Simple gave the Norse chieftain, Rollo, Upper Normandy in exchange for Norse allegiance and protection against further Norse raids, and conversion to Christianity by baptism. In reality, this established Normandy as a Norse colony under French rule, though the Norman dukes were practically independent of the French king.

The Rus' Kingdom

In Eastern Europe, the Rus' settlements were now well-established. Oleg, a relative of Rurik, seized power over Kiev from his own brother, and in doing this, established what would become the kingdom of the Kievan Rus', ruled by the Rurik dynasty. From his new position in Kiev, which controlled the Slavic areas' trade routes, Oleg was able to launch at least one attack on the wealthy capital of the Byzantine Empire, Constantinople. At the same time, the Byzantine emperor began to recruit elite Norse warriors exclusively, to serve as his personal guard, known as the Varangian Guard, to protect him from political attacks from within the Empire.

First churches are built in Scandinavia

850 — **Norsemen settle by the Thames near London, England**
The Hon Hoard

Norsemen raid in Spain, North Africa, Rhône Valley and Italy

860 —

The Rus' Kingdom is established by Oleg

The Great Heathen Army invades England

870 — **Harald Fairhair unites Norway**

Norsemen settle in Iceland

The Danelaw is established

880 —

890 — *The Gokstad Ship*

Borre style
c. 850 – 950

900 —

Norsemen attack Constantinople

910 —

Normandy is established by Rollo

Edward the Elder conquers the Southern Danelaw

920 —

930 —

Haakon the Good becomes king of Norway

Gorm the Old becomes king of Denmark

940 — *The Vårby Hoard*
The Vester Vedsted Hoard

The Terslev Hoard

Eric Bloodaxe becomes king of Northumbria
The Skaill Hoard

950 —

The Gnezdovo Hoard

Golden Age of the Gripping Beast

Development

If the Oseberg style saw innovation in, and a reimagination of the traditional Norse animal ornament, the Borre style represents a further, almost complete departure in many ways. While the traditional gripping beast took centre stage and became the principal animal form of the Borre style, the ribbon animal vanished almost entirely for the first time in Germanic and Norse tradition. Though we often do find the typical ribbon animal head in profile, with its neck tendril, it is mostly used as just a ribbon terminal or decorative afterthought. Instead of intertwining ribbon animals, the interlacing patterns were now often almost exclusively geometric. These framework patterns may have originated in a further development of the geometric framework of the preceding Broa and Oseberg styles. The spiral was among the new geometric features introduced, probably inspired by European vegetal scroll motifs, though often used to represent animal hip joints. The gripping beast was often used either in its entirety as a centrepiece of the composition, curled up in a pretzel-like knot, or appeared simply as a single head applied to the end of a ribbon in an interlacing pattern, such as the *ring-chain* ornament. The gripping beast often also appears with just a knot for its body, with ribbon terminals in the shape of the head and paws.

Dating

The Borre style is the first phase of Viking Age art that may be more accurately dated, based on a few coin finds in conjunction with metalwork in hoards.

Gripping Beast Pendants

Some of the most iconic Borre-style pieces are the pendants found across Scandinavia, which display a typical gripping beast with its ribbon body and squat, wide hips, curled up in a pretzel knot, gripping its own slender limbs and the surrounding circular frame with its four paws.

The Borre Harness Mounts

On the horse-harness mounts from a ship grave in Borre, from which this style got its name, we find the other trademark of the Borre style, the so-called ring chain. This is formed by juxtaposing geometric shapes, typically circles and rhombuses, which often terminate in the triangular head of a gripping beast. The ring-chain pattern schemes are not known from Scandinavian tradition or foreign models, and therefore may be a Scandinavian innovation. A variation of the ring chain, Gaut's ring chain, was widely used in the Norse regions of the British Isles, and is seen on many stone crosses, the most notable of which are those made by Gaut Bjørnson.

The Birka Penannular Brooch

The penannular brooch from Birka is an excellent example of a combination of all the Borre style characteristics. Ring chains, knots, gripping beast heads and even tiny heads of ribbon animals are all part of the composition.

Distribution

The expansion and new settlements of the Norse are well-reflected in the distribution of Borre-style artefacts. The style is also the earliest to be found outside of Scandinavia. Not only do we find items made by the Norse in the Borre style, but the style also influenced the local styles of the settled regions, and the style itself represents a stage of decorative eclecticism. The style was especially popular in the British Isles, where it was picked up and combined with local trends. Although stone carving was virtually non-existent in Scandinavia, it was very common in the British Isles, and local artists integrated the Borre style in many works in stone.

Examples

Dateable

c. 850
Gilt silver pendants — the Hon Hoard
Hon, Buskerud, Norway.
Universitetets Oldsaksamling, Oslo, C719–51, 12210–11, 13451–54, 14473–4, 14616–17, 30259

c. 870
Tongue-shaped mount
Gokstad, Vestfold, Norway.
Universitetets Oldsaksamling, Oslo C10441a

c. 913 – 942
Gold disc brooch — the Vester Vedsted Hoard
Vester Vedsted, Jutland, Danmark.
Nationalmuseet, Copenhagen 18278, 18571, DNF 12/33

c. 940
Gilt silver pendants — the Vårby Hoard
Vårby, Södermanland, Sweden.
Historiska Museet, Stockholm SHM 456

c. 944
Silver pendants — the Terslev Hoard
Terslev, Zealand, Danmark.
Nationalmuseet, Copenhagen DNF 33/11, 35/11, 40/11, 46/11

c. 953 – 954
Pendants — the Gnezdovo Hoard
Gnezdovo, Smolensk, Rusland.
Gosudarstvennyj Ermitaž, Saint Petersburg 994

Undateable

Animal-head needle
Hedeby, Schleswig, Germany.
Archäologisches Landesmuseum Schleswig, Schleswig

Animal-head pendant
Sigtuna, Uppland, Sverige.
Historiska Museet, Stockholm SHM 27883

Bridle
Suputry, Rusland.
Gosudarstvennui Istoricheskii Muzei, Moskva.

Bronze dies
Hedeby, Schleswig, Germany.
Archäologisches Landesmuseum Schleswig, Schleswig

Cast silver disc brooch
Gotland, Sweden.
The British Museum, London 1901,0718.1

Circular brooch
Bjølstad, Heidal, Oppland, Norge.
Universitetets Oldsaksamling, Oslo C23005

Cruciform pattern filigree disc brooch
Finkarby, Taxinge, Södermanland, Sweden.
Historiska Museet, Stockholm

Equal-armed brooch
Elec, Upper Don, Russia.
Gosudarstvennyj Ermitaž, Saint Petersburg 997/1

Gaming board
Gokstad, Vestfold, Norway.
Universitetets Oldsaksamling, Oslo C10406

Gaut's Cross
Kirk Michael, Isle of Man.

Gilt bronze horse-harness mounts — the Borre Grave
Borre, Vestfold, Norway.
Universitetets Oldsaksamling, Oslo C1804

Gilt silver quatrefoil brooch
Rinkaby, Skåne, Sweden.
Historiska Museet, Stockholm SHM 4578

The Hiddensee Hoard
Hiddensee, Rügen, Germany.
Kulturhistorisches Museum Stralsund 1873: a–d, f–g, i, 450. 1874: 39 a–b, 91–92, 162,176

Horse-harness mounts
Björkö, Adelsö, Uppland, Sweden.
Statens Historiska Museum, Stockholm.
SHM 34000:Bj 644

Penannular brooch
Björkö, Adelsö, Uppland, Sweden.
Statens Historiska Museum, Stockholm.
SHM 34000:Bj 581

Round brooch
Björkö, Adelsö, Uppland, Sweden.
Statens Historiska Museum, Stockholm.
SHM 34000: Bj 967

Terslev-style pendant
Hedeby, Schleswig, Germany.
Archäologisches Landesmuseum Schleswig, Schleswig

The Værne Monastery Gold Hoard
Østfold, Norway.

Ship and gripping beast ornament
Randlev, Jutland, Denmark.
Nationalmuseet, Copenhagen

Jelling Style

c. 900 — 975

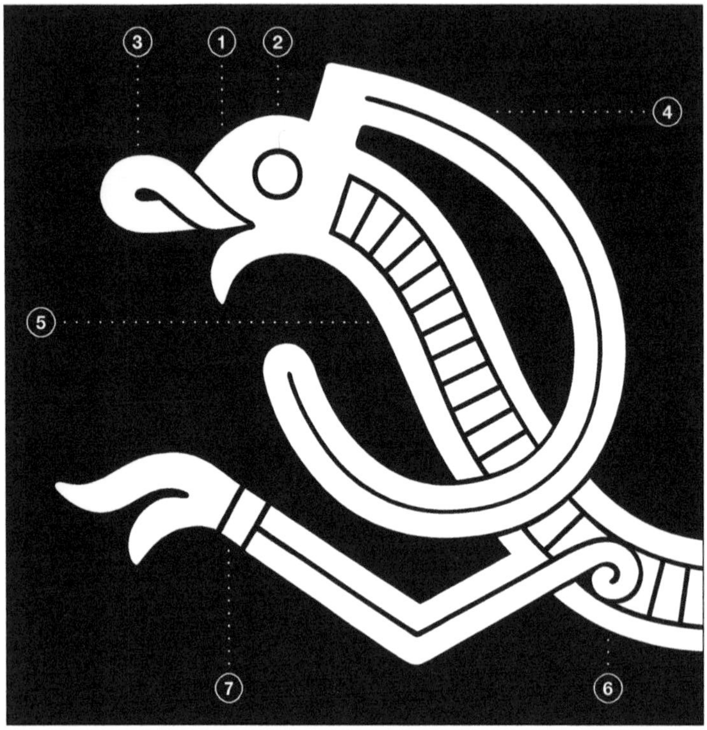

Shapes

1 Head in profile.
2 Round or almond-shaped eye.
3 Curled lip lappet.
4 Neck tendril.
5 Solid body.
6 Spirals representing hip joints.
7 Pellets intersecting limbs at joints.

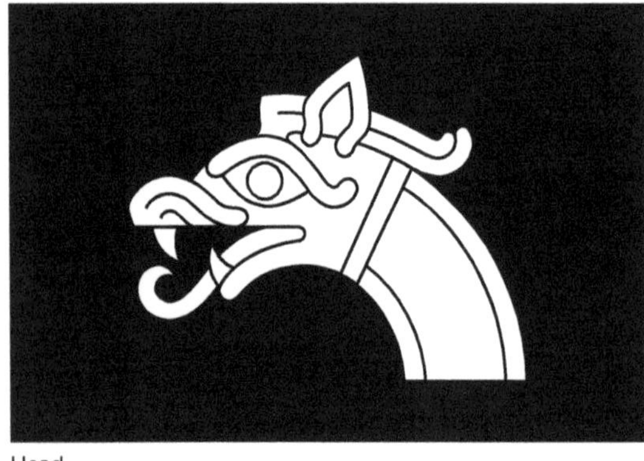

Head

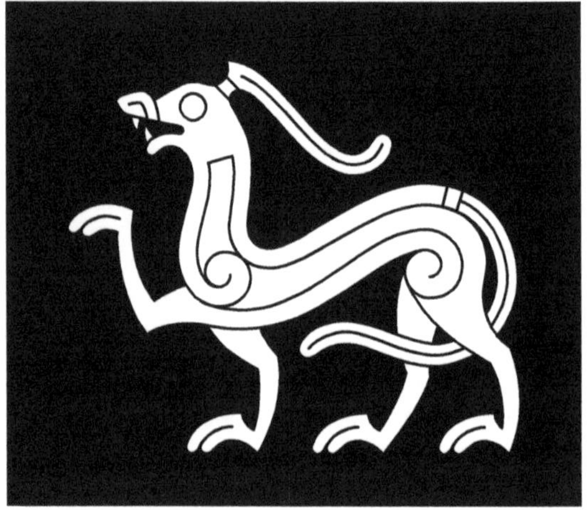

Body

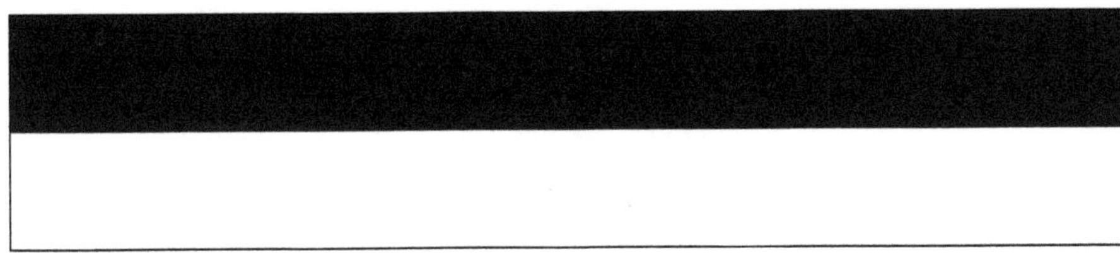

Outlines

Even outlines without tapering or indents.

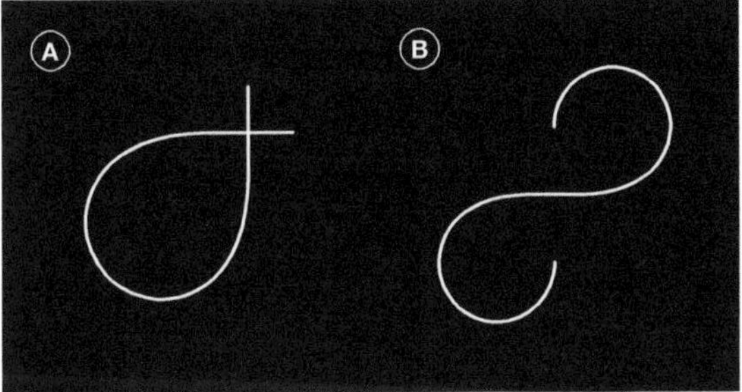

Flow

A mix of wavy and almost circular curves.

A Single loops.
B S-shapes.

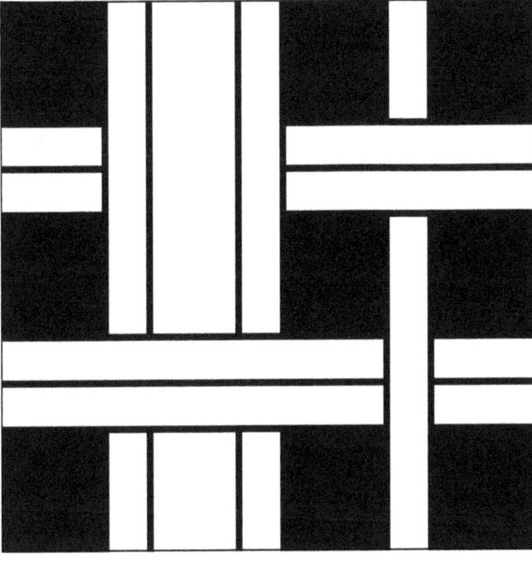

Pattern

- Restrained use of interlacing, with some visible background.
- Double contour.
- Single-strand ribbons.
- Double-strand ribbons.

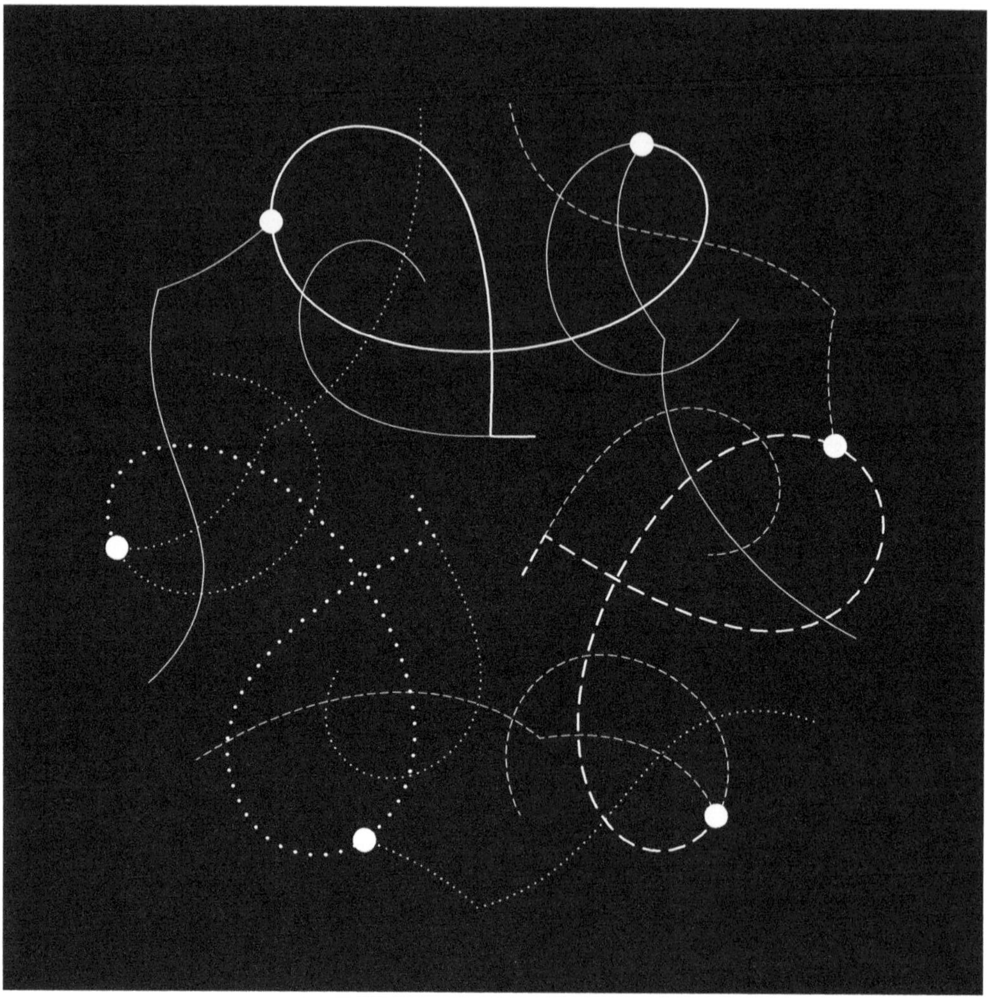

A

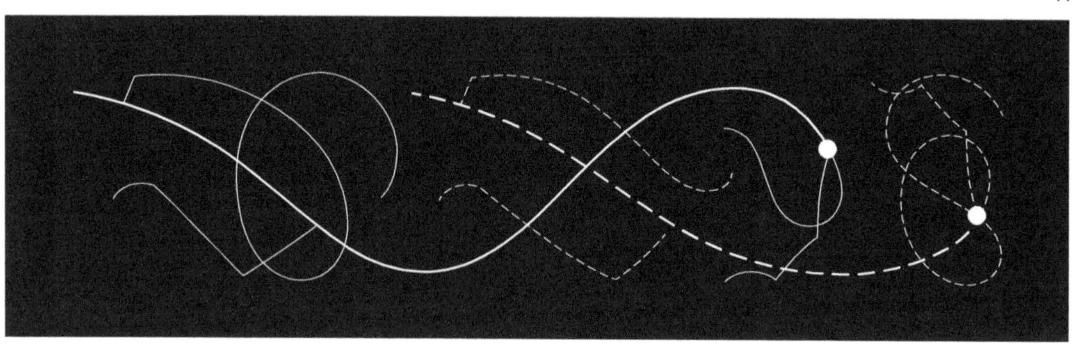

B

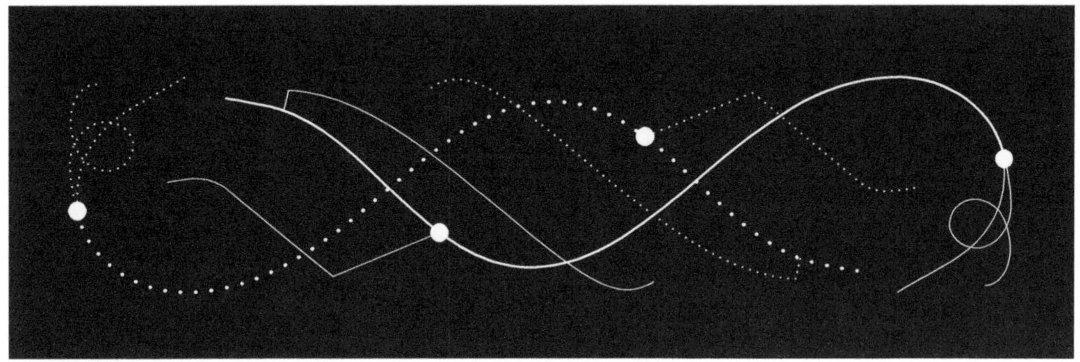

C

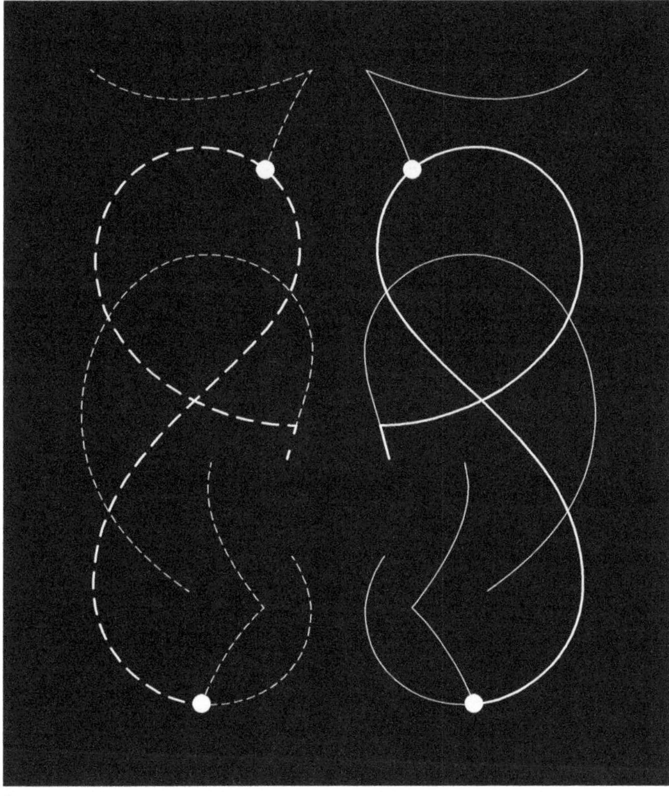

D

Composition

- Simple compositions of juxtaposed and overlapping S-shapes (B, C, D).
- Overlapping pretzel knots evenly distributed around the centre of a circular composition. (A).
- Mirrored S-shapes (D).

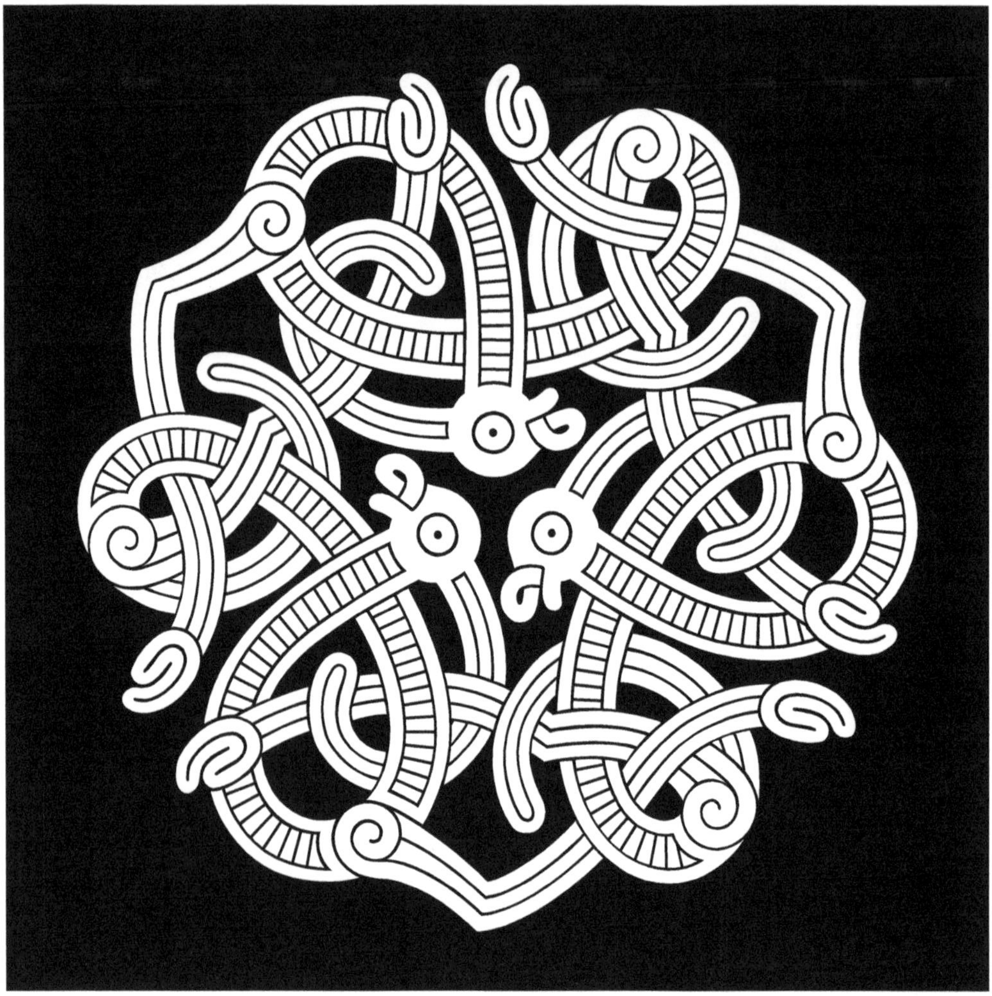

A

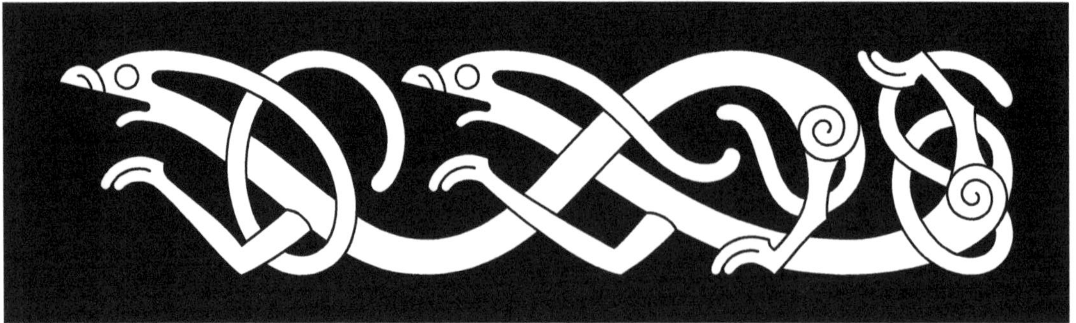

B

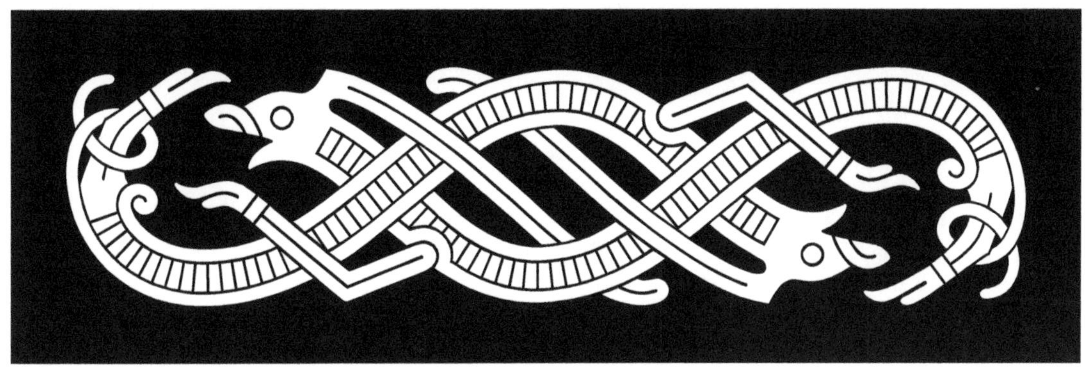

C

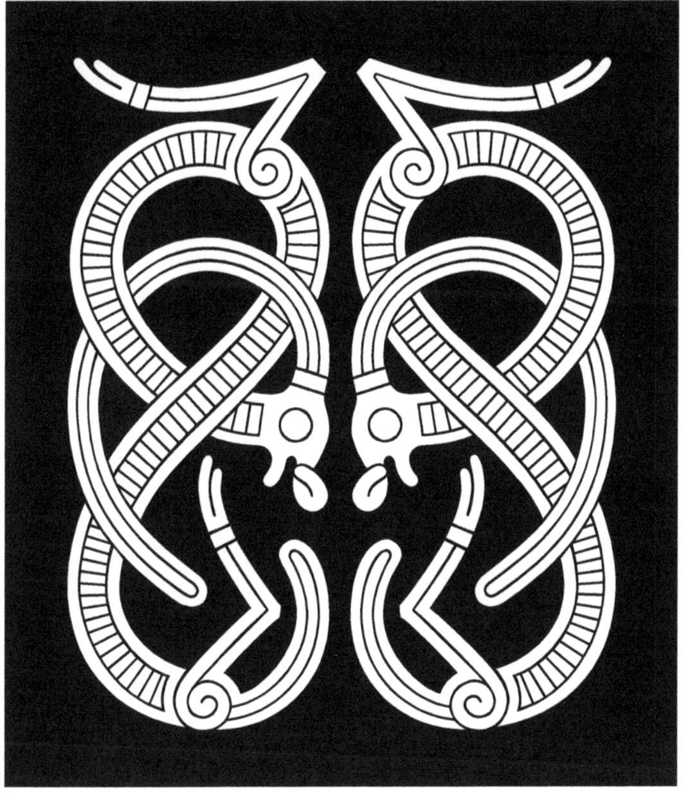

D

Motifs

- Ribbon animals, typically with striated bodies.

Rise of the Jelling Dynasty

English Control of the Danelaw

The Anglo-Saxon King Edward the Elder managed to take back most of the Danelaw except Northumbria, which remained under Norse rule. A few years later his son Eadred finally managed to gain control over and absorb Northumbria into the English Kingdom after the death of King Eric Bloodaxe, and in doing so ended the Norse reign in English territory.

The Jelling Dynasty

Power in Denmark began to concentrate in and around the aristocracy of the Jelling area, on the Jutland peninsula. Gorm the Old is the first historically recognised king of Denmark. His wife Thyra is mentioned on a number of runestones in the Jelling area, particularly on the Lesser Jelling Stone, which Gorm raised in her memory. It is believed that when Gorm died, he was buried in the chamber of the North Mound in Jelling, built by his son and successor, Harald Bluetooth. However, Gorm's remains were later moved from the mound to a final resting place under the wooden church built by Harald when he converted to Christianity.

The First Christian Norse King

After the death of Harald Fairhair, his son Haakon the Good returned to Norway to fight his half-brother, Eric Bloodaxe, over his claim to the throne. According to legend, Haakon was fostered by the Anglo-Saxon King Athelstan, son of Edward the Elder, as part of an agreement made with his father, Harald. In England, he was influenced by the Christian faith of the English people, which he brought back with him to Norway. Haakon gained the support of the Norwegian landowners by promising to cede the right to tax them claimed by his father. With his new-found support, he was able to force Eric to flee to the British Isles, where he eventually would be King of Northumbria for a few years before his death. Haakon later fought and was eventually defeated by Eric's sons, supported by Gorm the Old.

Bishoprics in Scandinavia

Several of the trading towns such as Hedeby and Aarhus became the seat of a bishop under the Archbishopric of Hamburg and Bremen.

The Holy Roman Empire

Following the death of Emperor Louis the Pious, the Frankish Empire was divided in three: West Francia, Middle Francia and East Francia. No emperor was appointed in the West for several years, until the crowning of the Saxon king, Otto I.

890 *The Gokstad Ship*

900

Norsemen attack Constantinople

910

Normandy is established by Rollo

Edward the Elder conquers the Southern Danelaw

920

930

Jelling style
c. 900 – 975

Haakon the Good becomes king of Norway

Gorm the Old becomes king of Denmark

940 *The Vårby Hoard*
The Vester Vedsted Hoard

The Terslev Hoard

Eric Bloodaxe becomes king of Northumbria
The Skaill Hoard

950

The Gnezdovo Hoard

Eadred conquers the Northern Danelaw
Temporary end of Norse reign over England

Harald Bluetooth becomes king of Denmark
960 And regains control over Norway the following year
The Jelling North Mound

Harald Bluetooth Christianises Denmark
The Greater Jelling Stone

970 *The Mammen Grave*

Otto II occupies Hedeby
Until 983 when Harald Bluetooth regains control

980 **The ring fortresses are built in Denmark**

Greenland is colonised by Norsemen

Bishops are inserted in Denmark

Vladimir the Great baptises the Kievan Rus'

990

Sweyn Forkbeard collects 1st Danegeld

Return of the Ribbon Animal

Development

With the Jelling style begins a revival of the ribbon animal, eventually pushing the motif of the gripping beast into oblivion. Though often executed in fairly simple, juxtaposed and overlapping S-shaped layouts, and still drawing heavily on the highly geometric interlacing patterns of the preceding Borre style, such as the pretzel knot and chain patterns, the Jelling style is largely a return to the Norse traditions of animal ornament reminiscent of the Broa style, and even the earlier Germanic styles. The Jelling style ribbon animal was further developed in the subsequent styles, and various iterations continued to be in fashion right up to the end of the Viking Age. Compared to the subsequent iterations of the ribbon animal in the Mammen, Ringerike and Urnes styles, the anatomy of the Jelling animal is relatively simple and formalised, with its equal-width ribbon body, neck tendril and curly upper lip-lappet. All these components constitute the backbone of the style, and spill over into the subsequent styles, with the addition of their individual stylistic traits. And though the execution of the Jelling style may vary, and sometimes seem superficially unrelated, when one looks closer, the underlying structure is often revealed as strictly conventional. Thus, the style both pays tribute to the ribbon animal tradition of the past, and establishes the new tradition of future Norse animal ornament.

Disc Brooches and Circular Pendants

The early Jelling style is often found on disc brooches and circular pendants beside jewellery of approximately the same type, featuring Borre style decorations. The Jelling style designs often make use of Borre style compositional schemes, but instead of gripping beasts, they feature ribbon animals with their heads in profile, and neck tendrils.

The Jelling Cup

This style got its name from a small cup that displays two overlapping S-shaped ribbon animals, found in the burial chamber of the North Mound of the Jelling monument site, and it is believed to have been part of the grave goods that accompanied Gorm the Old after his death.

Horse-Harness Bows

The three horse-harness bows found in Mammen, Jutland and Søllested, Funen, display more elaborate and figurative ornaments, while featuring some of the Jelling style trademarks, such as the curled lip lappet and single neck tendril. They seem as though they may be later developments of this style, on the cusp of a transition into the Mammen style.

Distribution

Like the preceding Borre style, we find the Jelling style in all areas where the Norse went at the time, from the British Isles through Eastern and Western Europe. There was no widespread tradition of stone carving in Scandinavia at this time, but a few stone monuments on the British Isles and the Isle of Man display motifs that clearly derive from the contemporary Scandinavian style. The craftsmen of the British Isles already worked with animal patterns and interlacing, which made a mutual influence between the Anglo-Saxon style and the Scandinavian style very easy.

Examples

Dateable

c. 890 (the ship)
Animal-head tent pole – the Gokstad Grave
Gokstad, Vestfold, Norway.
Universitetets Oldsaksamling, Oslo C10408

c. 945 – 946
The Skaill Hoard
Skaill, Orkney.

c. 958 – 959
The Jelling Cup – the Jelling North Mound
Jelling, Jutland, Denmark.
Nationalmuseet, Copenhagen CCCLXXII

Undateable

Animal-head horse-harness bow terminal
(site not registered) Denmark.
Nationalmuseet, Copenhagen 5254

Animal-head strap ends
Jelling, Jutland, Denmark.
Nationalmuseet, Copenhagen JL/301

Bronze die patrice
Mammen, Jutland, Denmark.
Nationalmuseet, Copenhagen C1067

Bronze mount
Gryta, Haram, Norway.

Bronze scabbard-terminal mount
Astala i Kokemäki, Satakunta, Finland.
Kansallismuseo, Helsinki 8338:39

Bronze strap end
Björkö, Adelsö, Uppland, Sweden.
Historiska Museet, Stockholm
SHM 34000:Bj 37

Oval brooch
Morberg, Røyken, Buskerud, Norway.
Universitetets Oldsakssamling, Oslo C21438a

Rectangular silver brooch
Ödeshög, Östergötland, Sweden.
Historiska Museet, Stockholm SHM 5671

Silver disc brooch
Nonnebakken, Fyn, Denmark.
Nationalmuseet, Copenhagen C6271

Gilt silver pendant
Vårby, Södermanland, Sweden.
Historiska Museet, Stockholm SHM 4516

Small disc brooch
Birka, Uppland, Sweden.
Historiska Museet, Stockholm

Silver filigree disc brooch – the Tråen Hoard
Tråen, Buskerud, Norway.

Tongue-shaped bronze brooch
Birka, Uppland, Sweden.
Historiska Museet, Stockholm SHM 5208

Tongue-shaped mount
Gokstad, Vestfold, Norway.
Universitetets Oldsaksamling, Oslo C24239c

Trefoil brooch
Blaker, Lom, Oppland, Norway.
Universitetets Oldsakssamling, Oslo C6743

Two horse-harness bows
Mammen, Jutland, Denmark.
Nationalmuseet, Copenhagen C1063

Two tongue-shaped mounts
Kornsá, Northwestern Region, Iceland.
Nationalmuseet, Reykjavík 1780–82

Horse-harness bow
Søllested, Odense, Denmark.
Nationalmuseet, Copenhagen 25581

Mammen Style

c. 950 — 1025

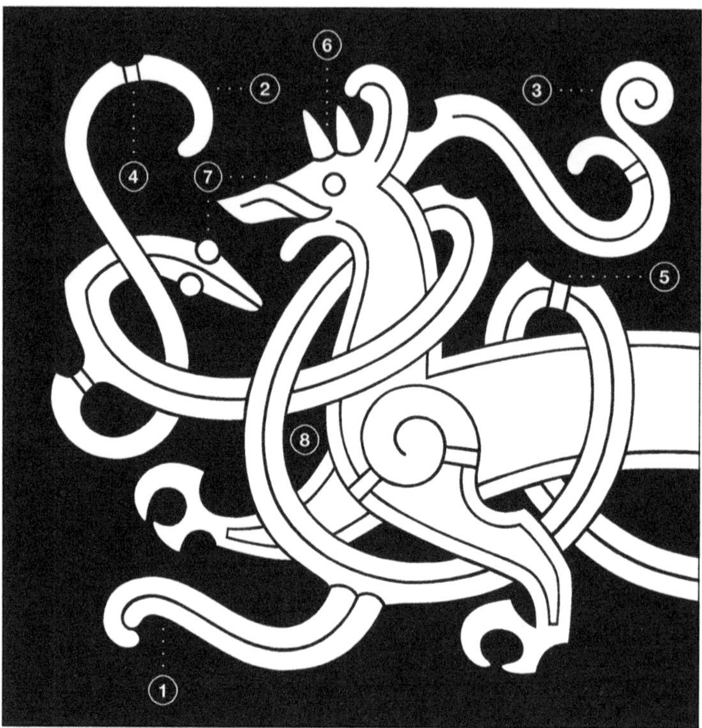

Shapes

1 Long and wavy S-shaped tendrils.
2 Loosely scrolled tendril terminals.
3 Spirals as tendril terminals.
4 Pellets intersecting ribbons.
5 Concave indents.
6 Head in profile.
7 Round or almond-shaped eye.
8 Spiral hip joints.

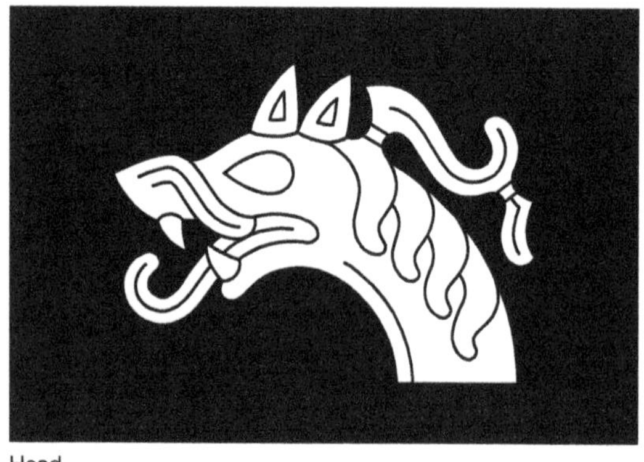

Head

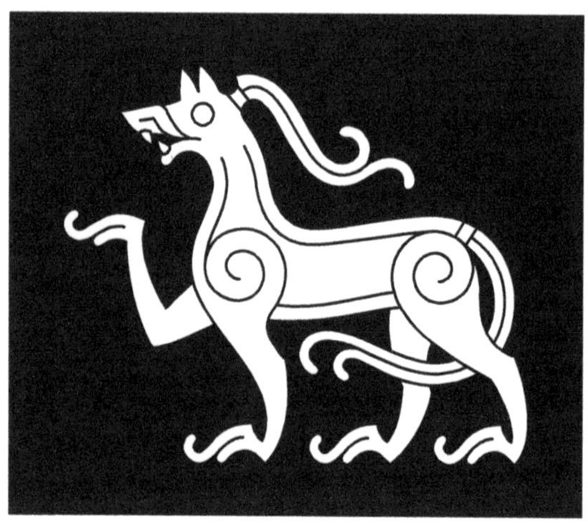

Body

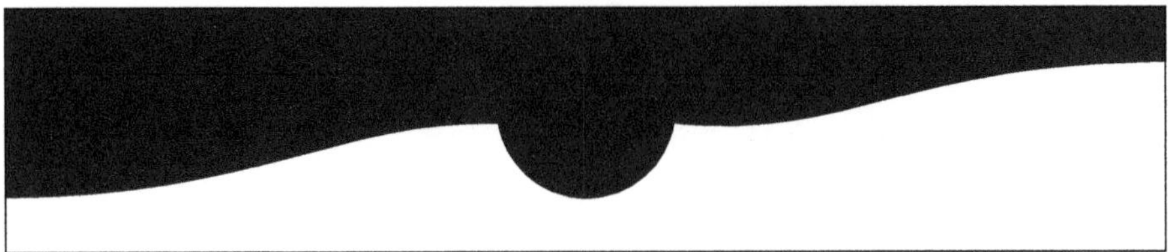

Outlines

Curvy outlines with kinks and frequent indents.

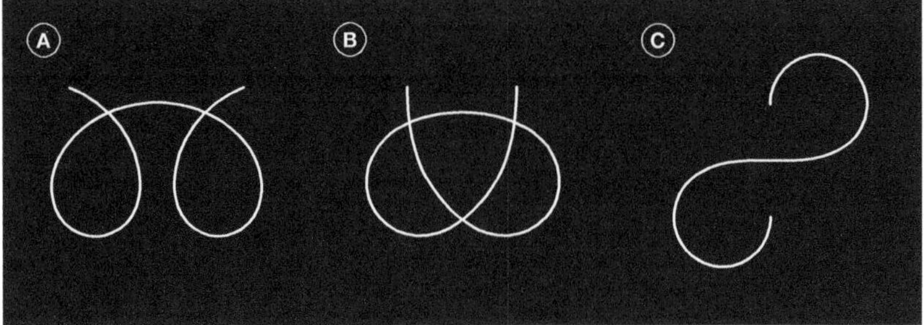

Flow

Flowing loose and wavy curves.

A Curly loops.
B Pretzel knots.
C S-shapes.

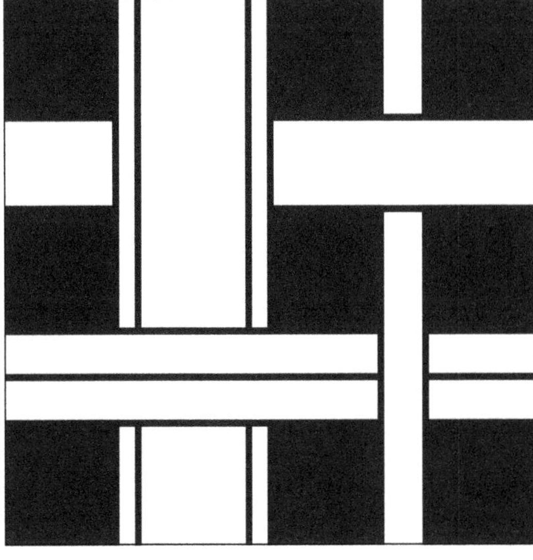

Pattern

- Semi-open interlacing with some visible background.
- Double contour.
- Single-strand ribbons.
- Double-strand ribbons.

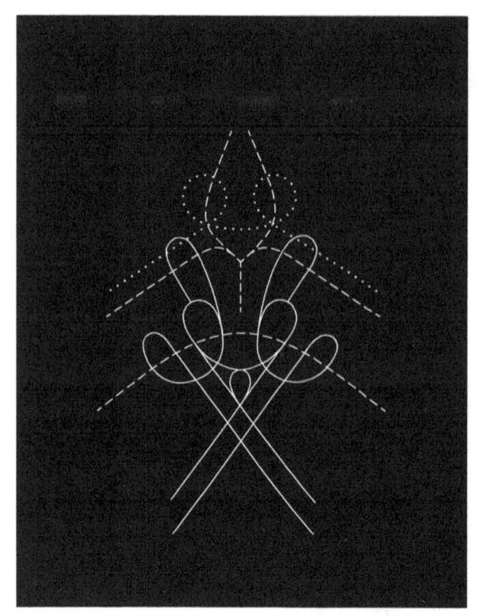

A

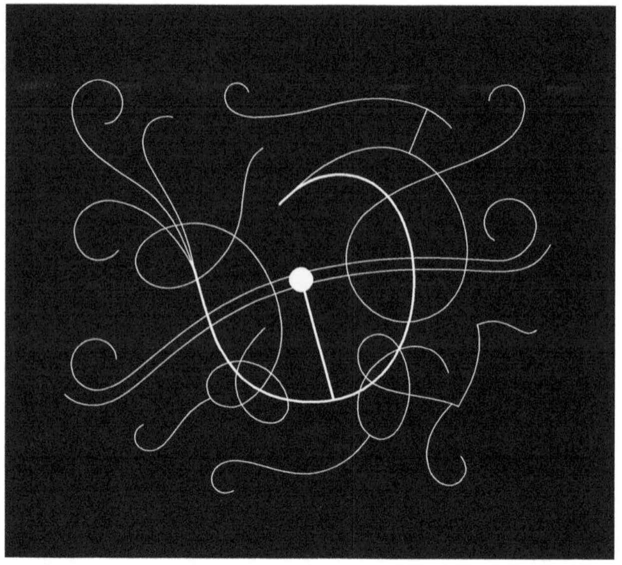

B

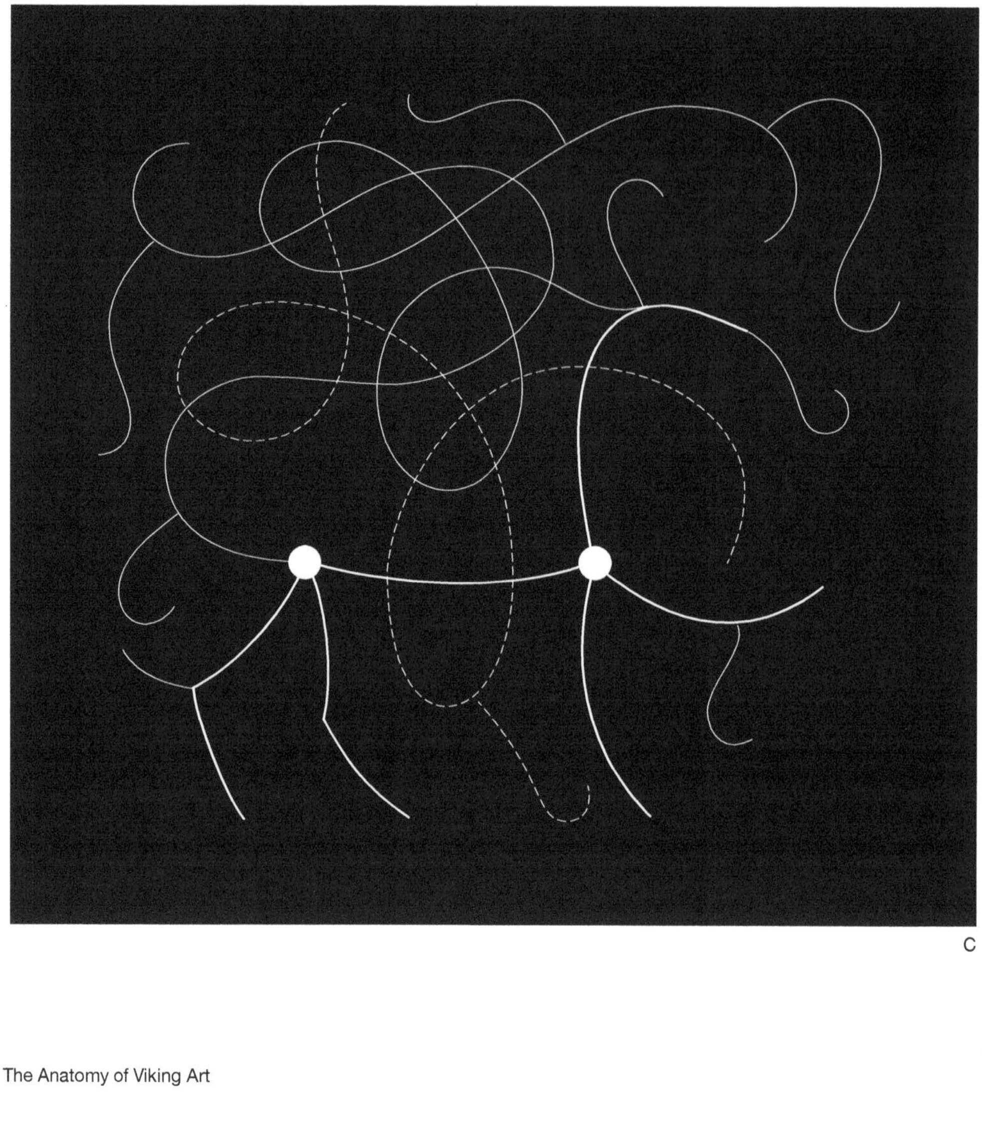

C

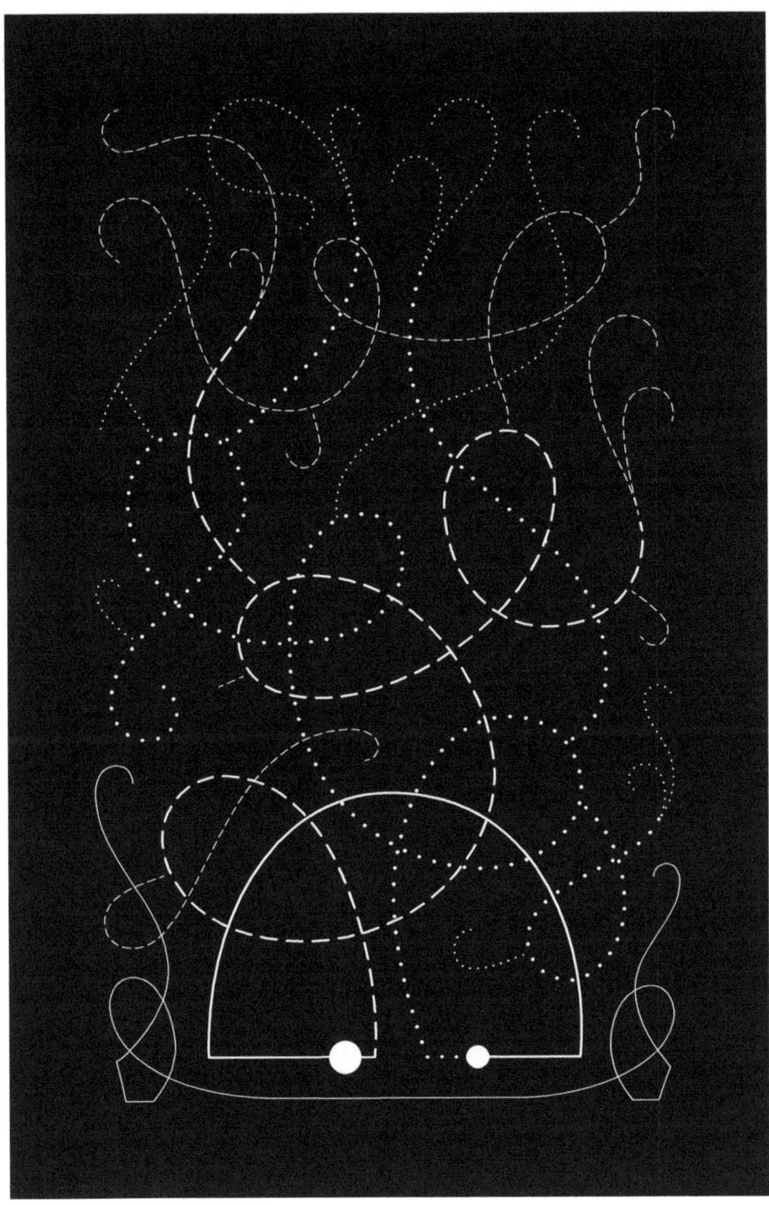

D

Composition

- Single motifs (A, B, C).
- Loosely flowing compositions without axes and symmetry (B, C, D).
- Additive principles.
- Stem and tendril ribbons often have the same width.

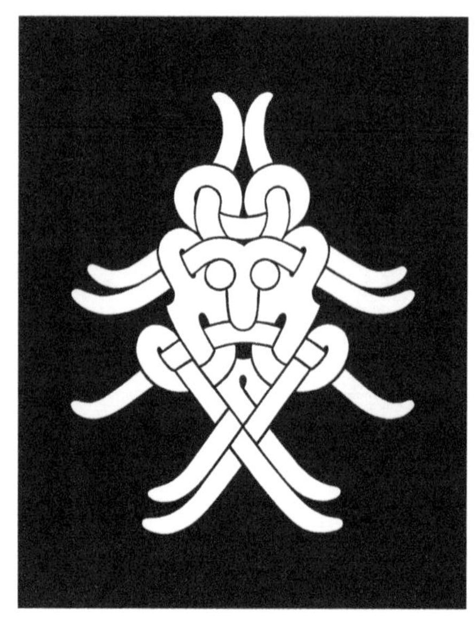

A

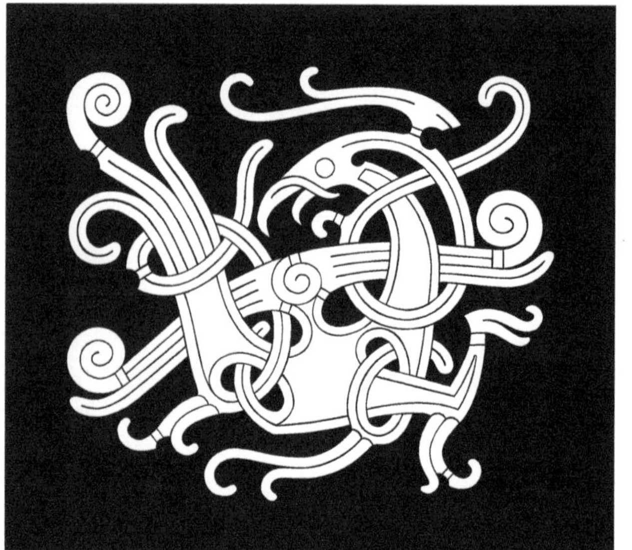

B

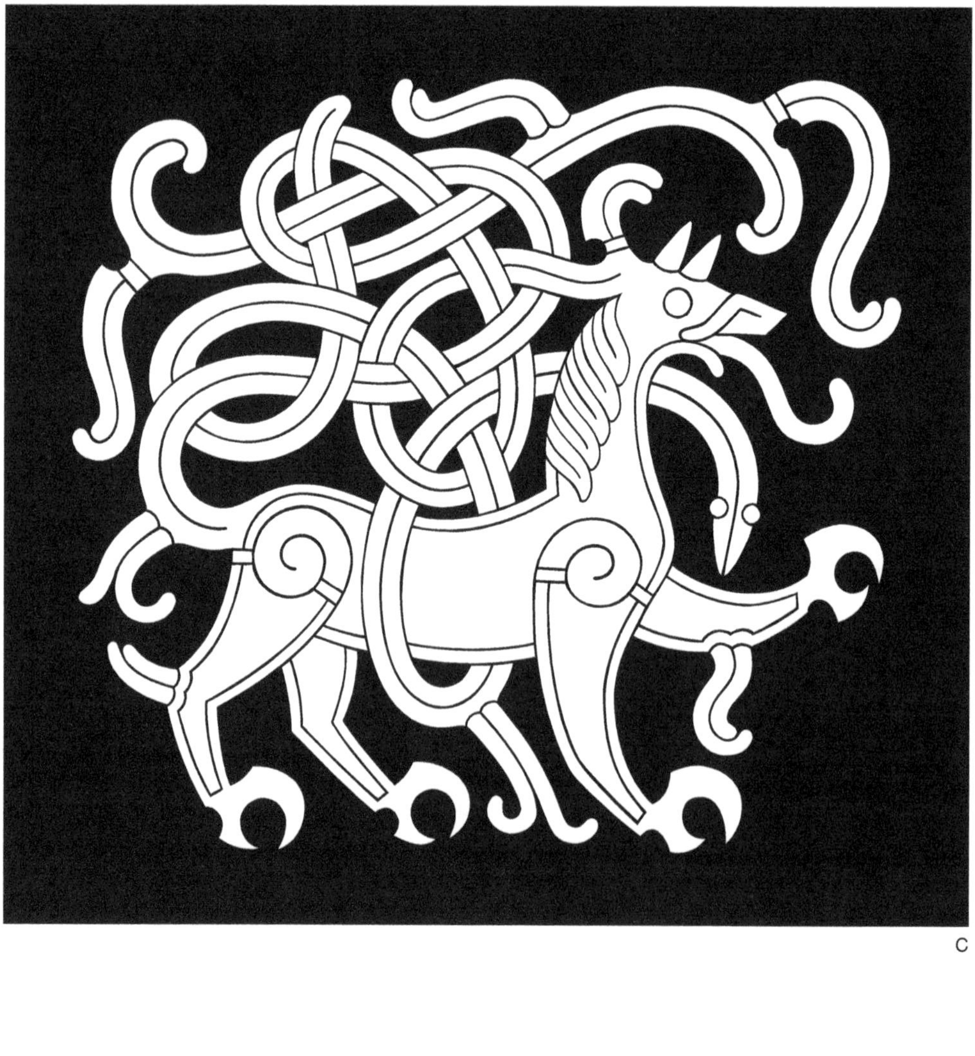

C

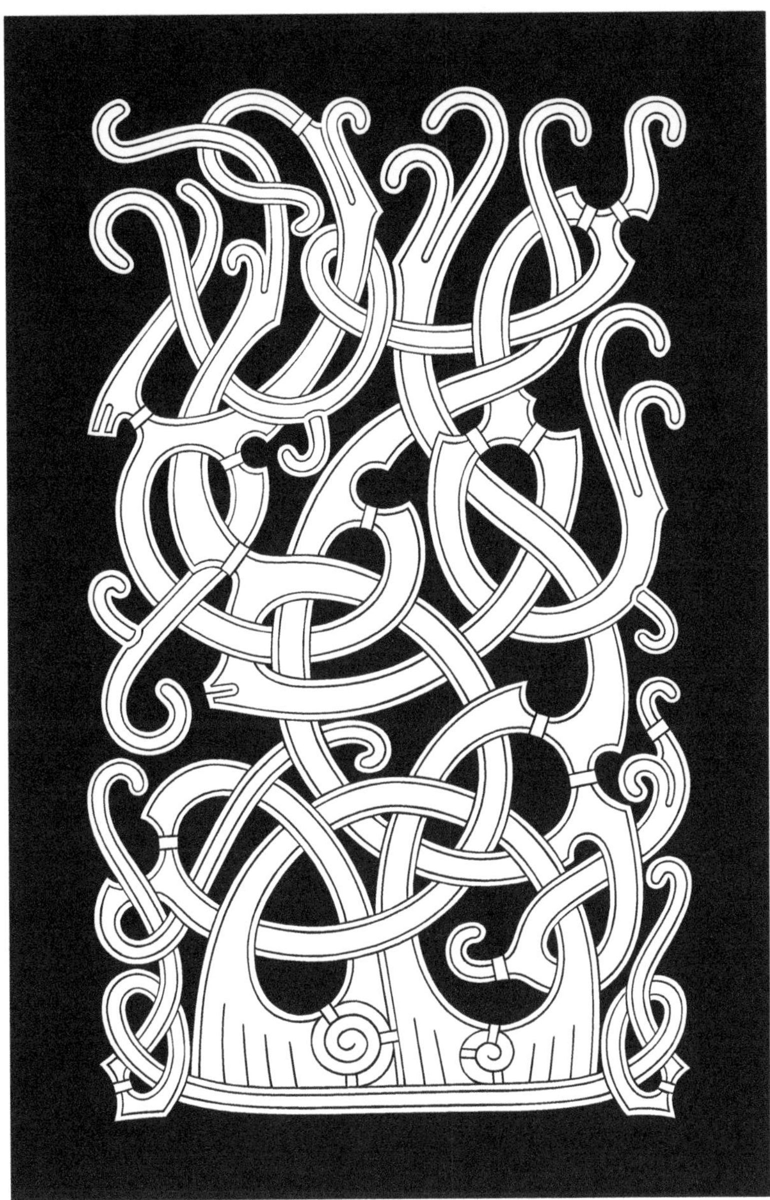

D

Motifs

- Great beast motifs, which are combinations of a mammalian carnivore and one or more serpents intertwined in battle (C).
- Mammals, typically carnivores (C).
- Serpents (C).
- Birds (B).
- Masks (A).
- Vegetal ornaments (D).

Christianisation of the Norse

The Conversion of Denmark

When Gorm the Old died, his son, Harald Bluetooth, became king of Denmark and acquired power over Norway a few years later. The joint ruler of the empire just south of the Dannevirke, Otto II, was keen on Christianising the Norse regions, by a violent military crusade if necessary. This threat forced Harald to convert, and to make Christianity Denmark's new religion. To communicate this point, he erected the Greater Jelling Stone, with its runic inscription that states that Harald united all Denmark, and converted the Danes. To further secure his status and control of the kingdom, he built a number of ring fortresses throughout the territory of Denmark, and fortified the Jelling monument site, the royal centre of power. Harald's display of power may have prevented Otto II from conquering Denmark, but after his father, Otto the Great, died, making him the sole ruler, he captured Hedeby, which was a tremendous blow to Harald. Otto II then suddenly died, and as his three-year-old son was the only legitimate heir, this left the empire in a state of complete political crisis. This led to Harald regaining control over Hedeby that same year. However, Harald's victory was short-lived, as he was then killed by his son, Sweyn Forkbeard, who took control of the kingdom.

The Conversion of the Rus'

After a period of exile in Sweden, Vladimir the Great of the Rurik dynasty returned to Novgorod with a Varangian army, took back control of the Rus' Kingdom from his brother, and soon after consolidated his rule of a sizeable Kievan territory. He was baptised, and Christianised all the Kievan Rus'.

The Conversion of Norway and Iceland

The heir to the Norwegian throne, Olaf Tryggvason, who was chief of Vladimir's men-at-arms while exiled from Norway, joined forces with Sweyn Forkbeard to lead an attack on England with a fleet of 90 ships, and collected the first Danegeld. They later returned to collect the second Danegeld, and as part of the treaty with King Æthelred the Unready, Olaf was baptised. After his success in England, Olaf returned to Scandinavia, successfully claimed the Norwegian throne and converted the Norwegians to Christianity. Iceland followed suit a few years later, through a somewhat democratic decision at the All-thing, mainly due to its dependence on trade connections with Norway. Olaf Tryggvason later fell foul of Sweyn Forkbeard by marrying Sweyn's already-married sister, Sigrid the Haughty. Sweyn then defeated Olaf in the Battle of Svolder with the support of Erik Jarl – who then became king of Norway – and Olof Skötkonung, who was the first Christian king of a united Sweden.

Colonisation of Greenland and Vinland

After all the inhabitable land in Iceland had been settled, Erik the Red established the first Norse colony on Greenland. His son Leif Eriksson (also known as Leif the Lucky) later discovered North America by accident, and attempted to colonise the land, which he called Vinland, but the settlement was ultimately a short and futile endeavour.

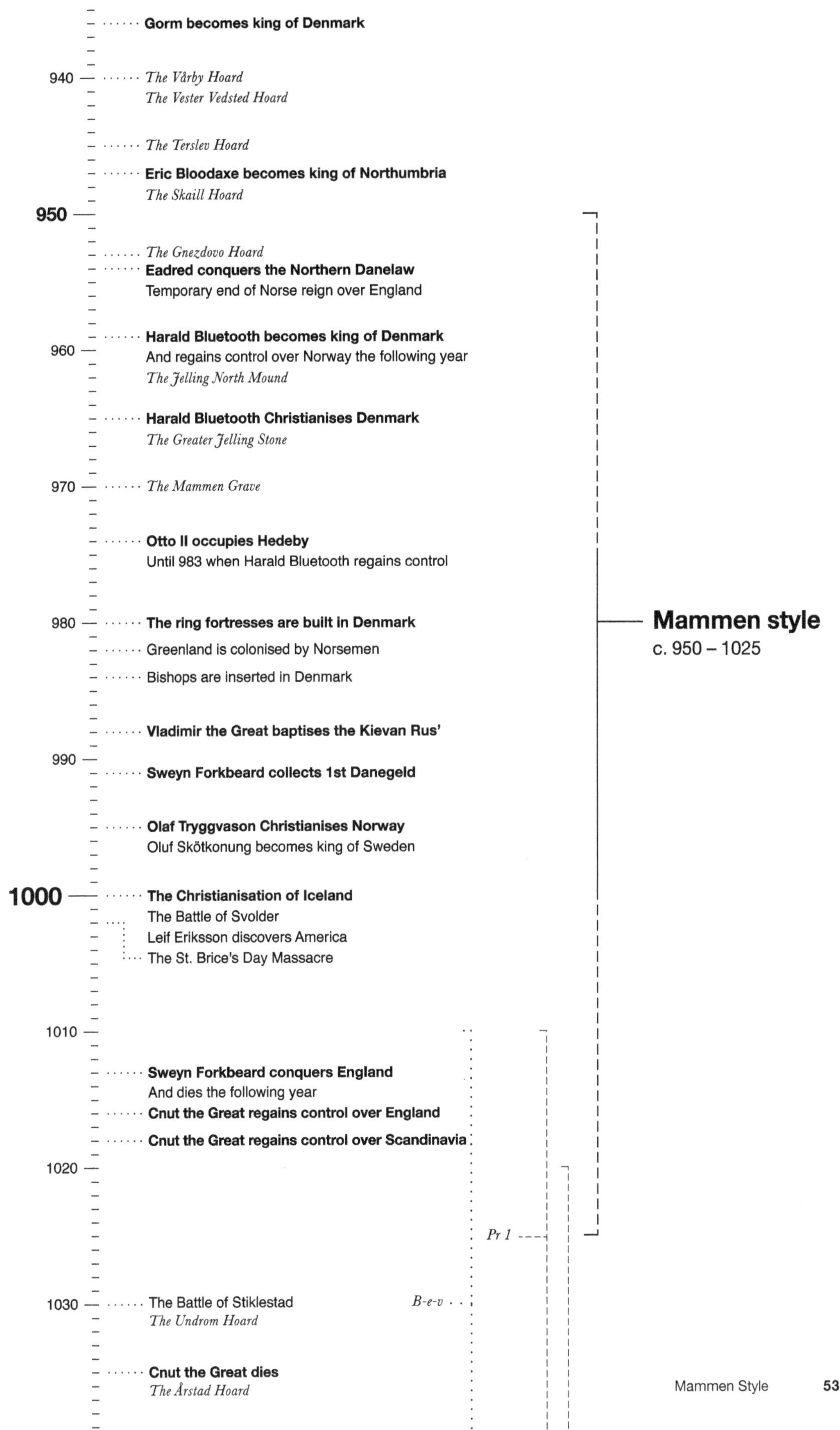

Gorm becomes king of Denmark
940
The Vårby Hoard
The Vester Vedsted Hoard
The Terslev Hoard
Eric Bloodaxe becomes king of Northumbria
The Skaill Hoard
950
The Gnezdovo Hoard
Eadred conquers the Northern Danelaw
Temporary end of Norse reign over England
Harald Bluetooth becomes king of Denmark
960
And regains control over Norway the following year
The Jelling North Mound
Harald Bluetooth Christianises Denmark
The Greater Jelling Stone
970
The Mammen Grave
Otto II occupies Hedeby
Until 983 when Harald Bluetooth regains control
980
The ring fortresses are built in Denmark
Greenland is colonised by Norsemen
Bishops are inserted in Denmark
Vladimir the Great baptises the Kievan Rus'
990
Sweyn Forkbeard collects 1st Danegeld
Olaf Tryggvason Christianises Norway
Oluf Skötkonung becomes king of Sweden
1000
The Christianisation of Iceland
The Battle of Svolder
Leif Eriksson discovers America
The St. Brice's Day Massacre
1010
Sweyn Forkbeard conquers England
And dies the following year
Cnut the Great regains control over England
Cnut the Great regains control over Scandinavia
1020
Pr 1
1030
The Battle of Stiklestad
B-e-v
The Undrom Hoard
Cnut the Great dies
The Årstad Hoard
1040
Pr 2
Mammen style
c. 950 – 1025

The Great Beast is Born

Development

The animals of the Mammen style are a stylistic continuation of the Jelling-style ribbon animal, though now with a more elaborate and often more naturalistic execution. The style was further inspired by Continental European influences, which may be seen in the introduction of more vegetal elements, such as vines, lobes and spirals. The interlacing patterns are developed in a less geometric, wavier and more flowing manner, reminiscent of vines.

Dating

The Christianisation of Scandinavia changed Norse burial customs. After the conversion, the dead were buried with very few artefacts, owing to the new religious beliefs, which rejected the importance of material goods accompanying the dead into the afterlife. The archaeological evidence comes mostly from the few hoards that may have been buried for safekeeping in times of conflict. Too few objects have been found in datable contexts to permit anything other than approximate dating.

The Greater Jelling Stone

The best-known example of the Mammen style is the Greater Jelling Stone, raised by Harald Bluetooth. On one of its three sides, we see for the first time the motif of the *great beast*, which came to be the most influential and widely used motif throughout the rest of the Viking Age. The motif consists of a large, four-legged animal, reminiscent of a lion or wolf, and a serpent, intertwined in battle. The motif builds heavily on Scandinavian artistic traditions while incorporating European influences. Therefore, it is difficult to determine the exact meaning of this image, but it may have been a symbol of royal or religious power, and may very well have been inspired by similar designs used in aristocratic environments in Continental Europe and the British Isles. On one of the other three sides of the stone we see a clear depiction of Christ, which was a highly untraditional motif in Scandinavia until then, though executed in an entirely traditional Norse style. The Greater Jelling Stone inspired copies throughout the Norse regions. However, the copies typically include only the great beast, and omit the image of Christ.

The Mammen Axe

The Mammen style got its name from the decorated axe head found among the rich grave goods of an aristocrat connected to the Jelling dynasty, buried just after the conversion of Denmark. One side is covered with a composition of waving foliate tendrils, and a bird in the same style occupies the other side.

The Bamberg and Cammin Caskets

Two of the most elaborate Mammen-style works are the casket from the Bamberg Cathedral, Germany, and the casket from the cathedral of Kamień Pomorski, Poland. Unfortunately, the latter was destroyed during World War II, though exact copies still exist. The Cammin casket is an excellent example of the integration of Norse artistic traditions and Christian iconography. Symbolic representations of the four evangelists appear on the lid and sides of the casket. John is represented by eagles, Luke by bulls depicted as four-legged animals with hooves, Matthew by a human mask and Mark by lions with clawed paws. Originally, the shrine may have contained a gospel or liturgical manuscript. Religious gifts of this kind played an essential role in the establishment of relationships between European and Norse rulers, and of generous donations to the Church.

Distribution

The Mammen style was widely popular throughout Scandinavia and the settled areas of Europe, especially the British Isles.

Examples

Dateable

c. 958 – 959
Wood carvings
– the Jelling North Mound
Jelling, Jutland, Denmark.
Nationalmuseet, Copenhagen CCCLXXVI

c. 965 – 975
The Greater Jelling Stone
Jelling, Jutland, Denmark.

c. 970 – 971
Axe head
– the Mammen Grave
Mammen, Jutland, Denmark.
Nationalmuseet, Copenhagen C133

Undateable

Antler handle
Køge, Zealand, Denmark.
Nationalmuseet, Copenhagen C18000

The Aarhus 3 Runestone
Aarhus, Jutland, Denmark.
Nationalmuseet, Copenhagen

The Bamberg Casket
Bamberg Cathedral, Bayern, Germany.
Bayerisches Nationalmuseum, Munich.

Bone cylinder
Årnes, Møre og Romsdal, Norway.
Trondheim Kgl. Norske Videnskabers Selskab Museet.

Bone disc
London, England.
The British Museum, London.

The Cammin Casket
Kamień, Pomorski, Poland.
(destroyed during WWII)

Gilt bronze plate
Aarhus, Jutland, Denmark.
Aarhus Museum, Aarhus.

The Léon Antler Box
León, Spain.
León SP 27-1-11A4

Lower guard of an antler sword hilt
Sigtuna, Uppland, Sweden.

Odd's Cross
Kirk Braddan, Isle of Man.

The Skårby 1 Runestone
Skårby, Scania, Sweden.

St Stephen's Sword
Prague, the Czech Republic.

Thorleif's Cross
Kirk Braddan, Isle of Man.

Ringerike Style

c. 1000 – 1075

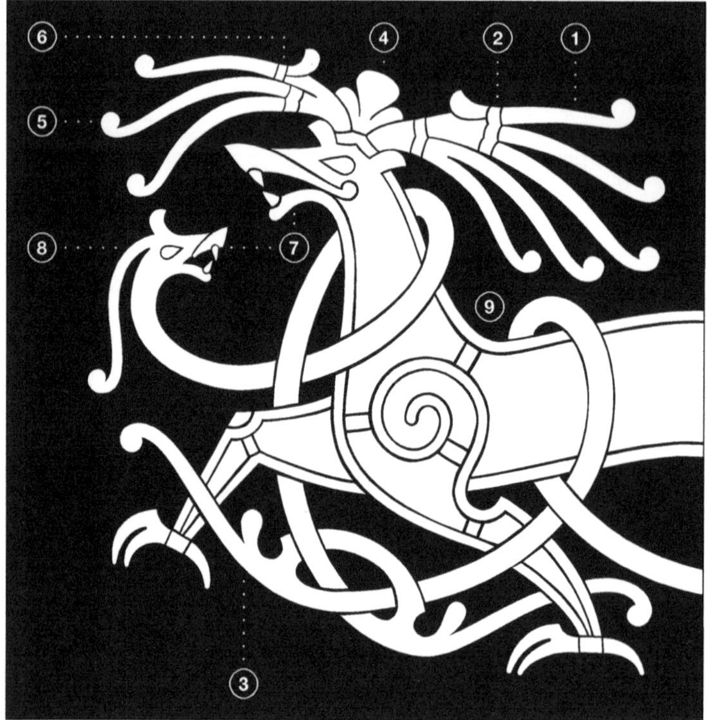

Shapes

1 Slim, short tendrils.
2 Clusters of fanned-out tendrils.
3 Tendrils with a single lobe.
4 Lobes with alternating side-lobes.
5 Tightly scrolled tendril terminals.
6 Pellets intersecting ribbons.
7 Head in profile.
8 Almond-shaped eye.
9 Spirals representing hip joints.

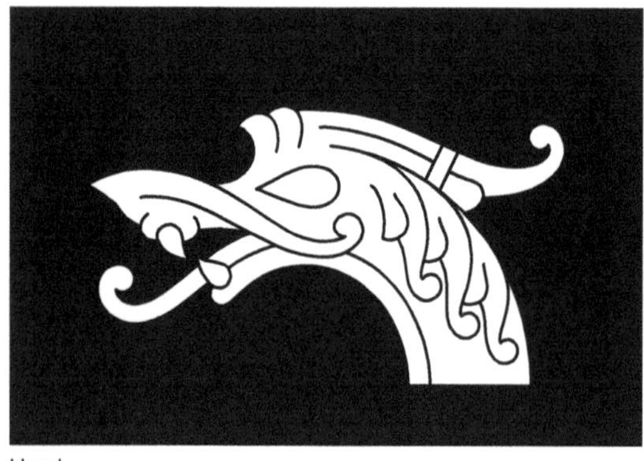

Head

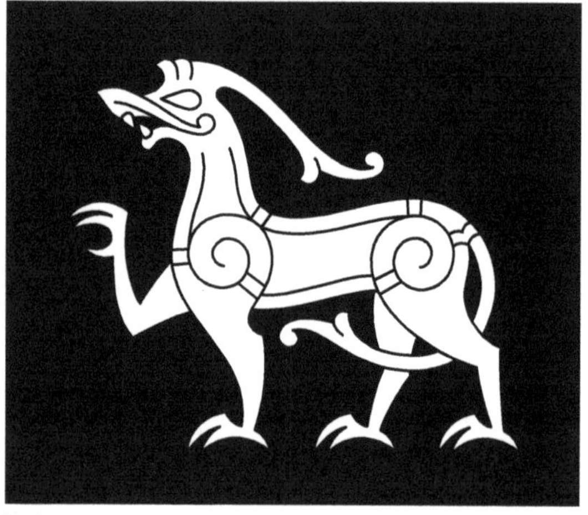

Body

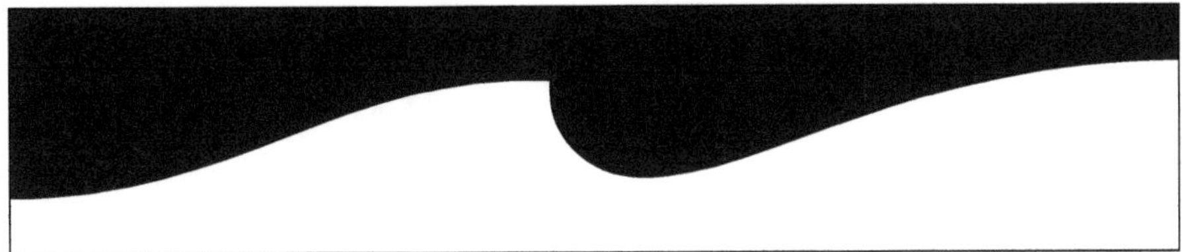

Outlines

Curvy outlines with occasional kinks and indents.

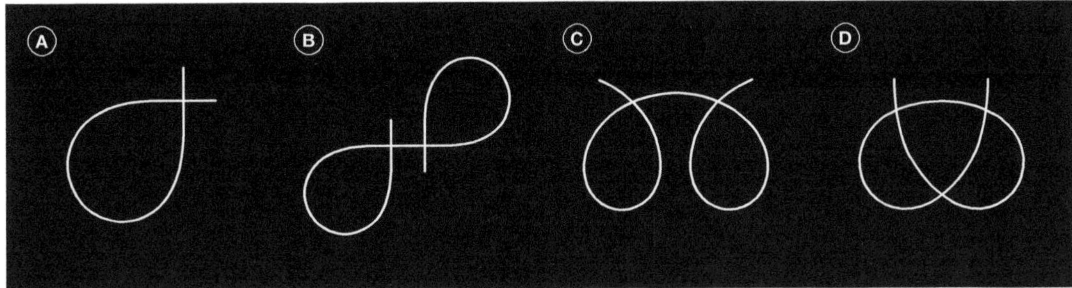

Flow

Taut curves looping in only one direction.

A Single loops.
B Figure-of-eight loops.
C Curly loops.
D Pretzel knots.

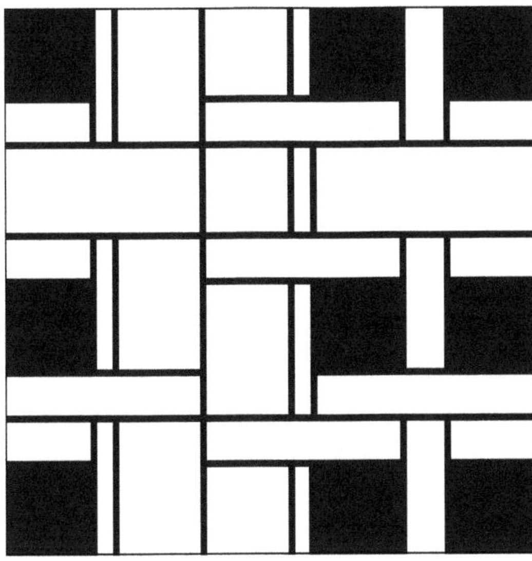

Pattern

- Semi-tight interlacing with some visible background.
- Double contours may appear.
- Single-strand ribbons.
- Double-strand ribbons may appear.
- Tight and more layered interlacing breaks ribbons into tile-like segments.

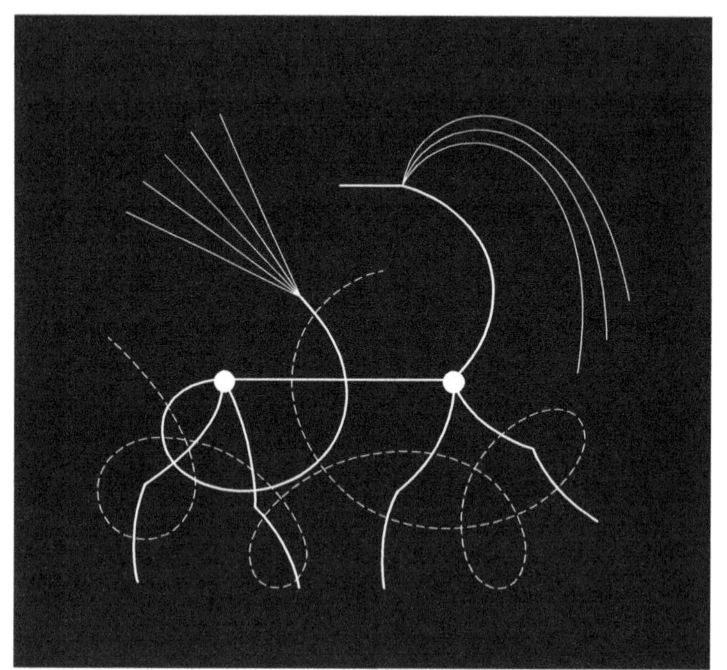

A

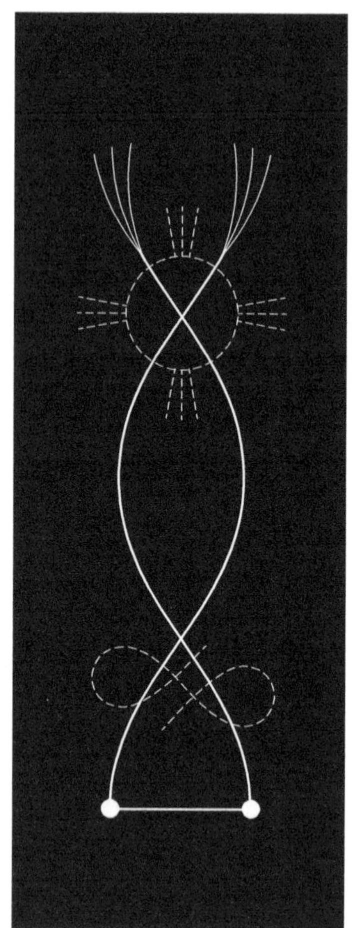

B

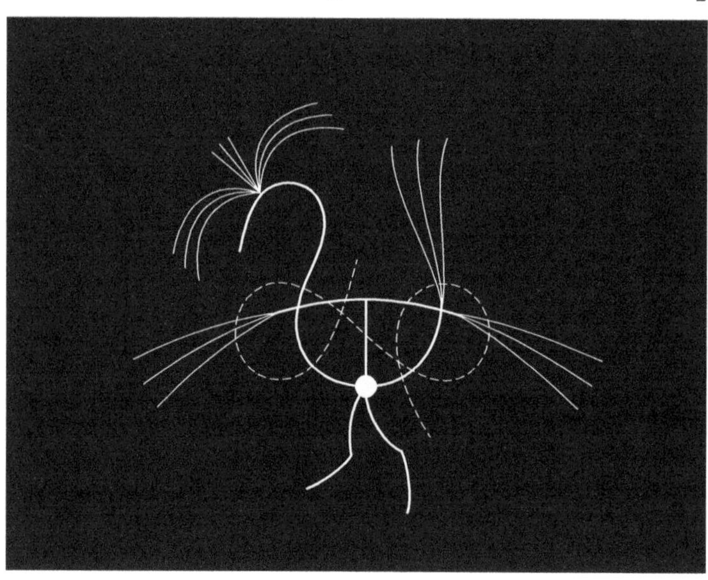

C

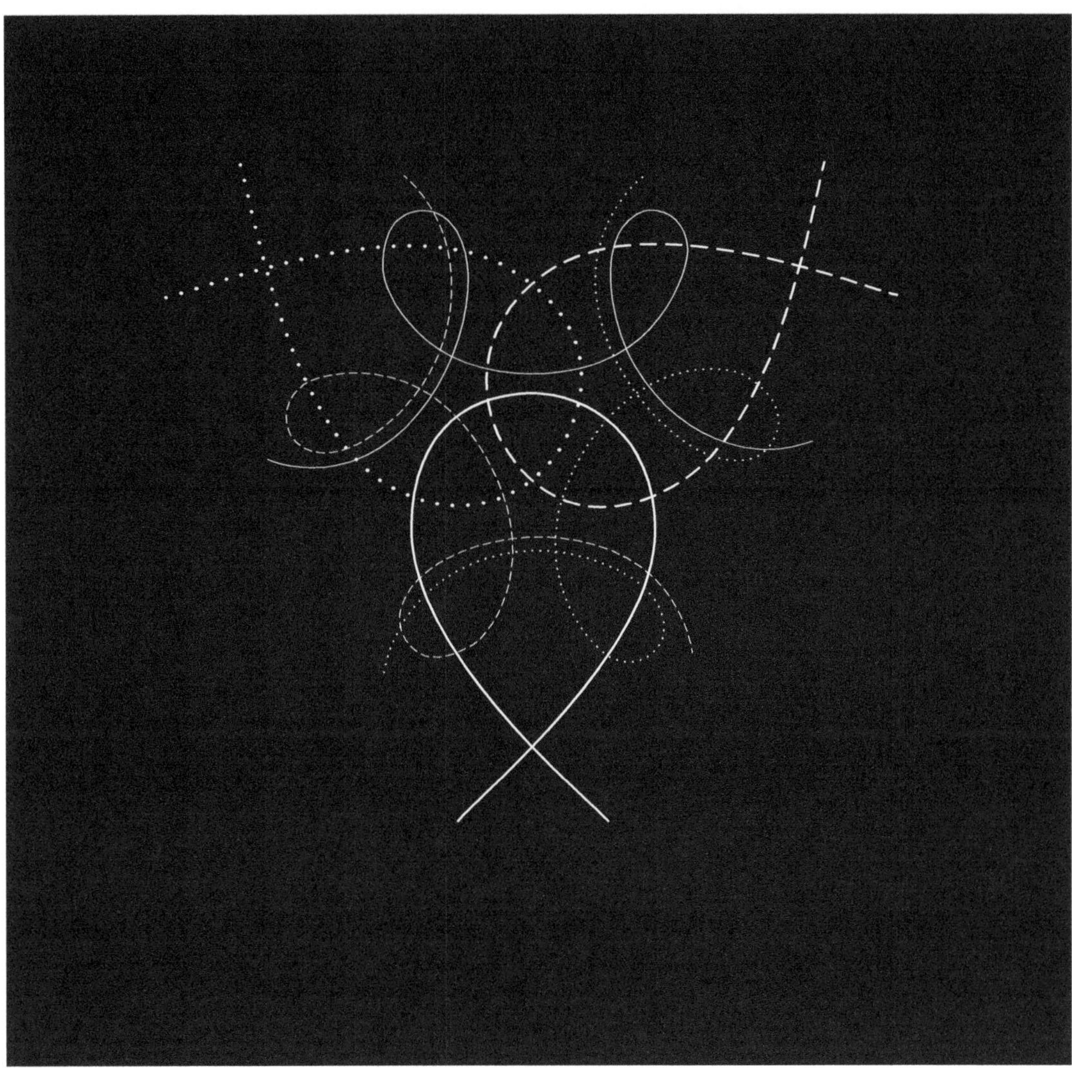

D

Composition

- Single motifs (A, C).
- Tauter compositions.
- Axes and symmetry (B, C, D).
- Additive principles, i.e. clusters of tendrils (A, B, C).
- Stem and tendril ribbons usually have different widths (A, B, D).

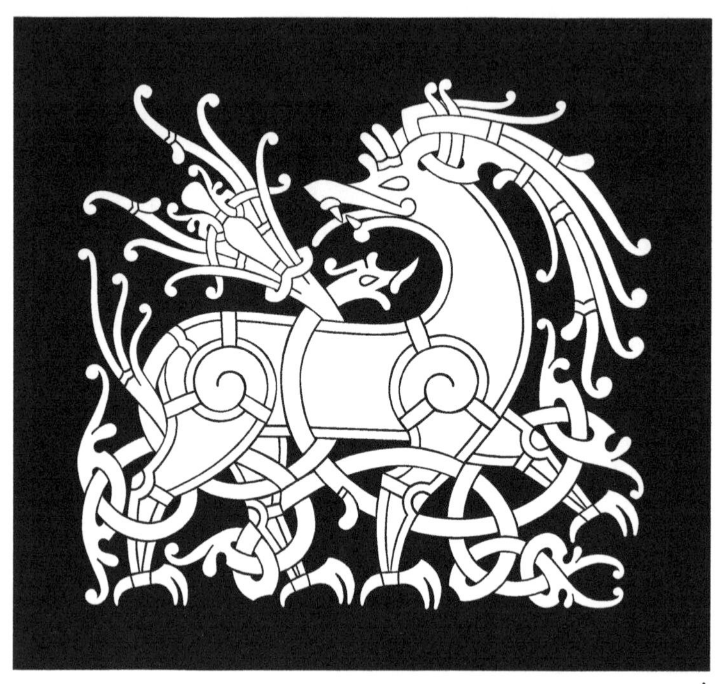

A

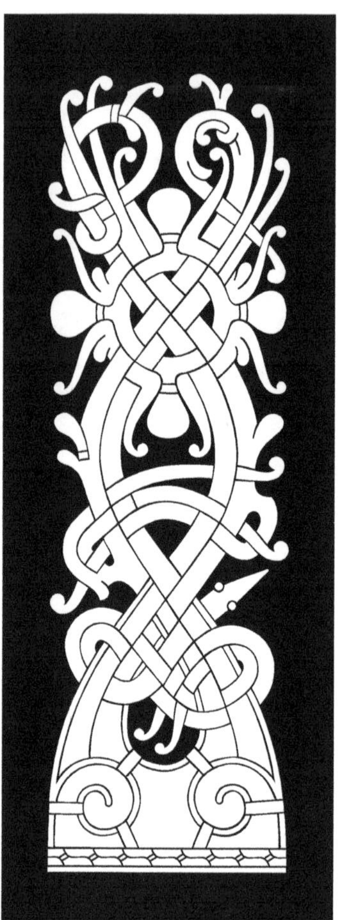

B

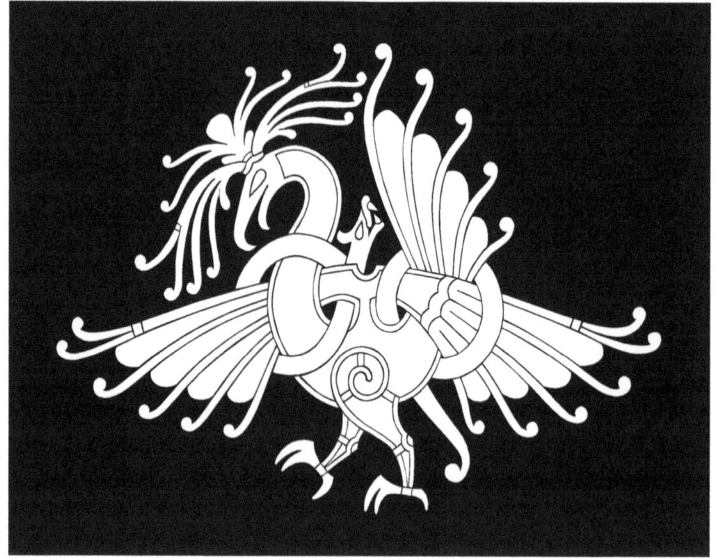

C

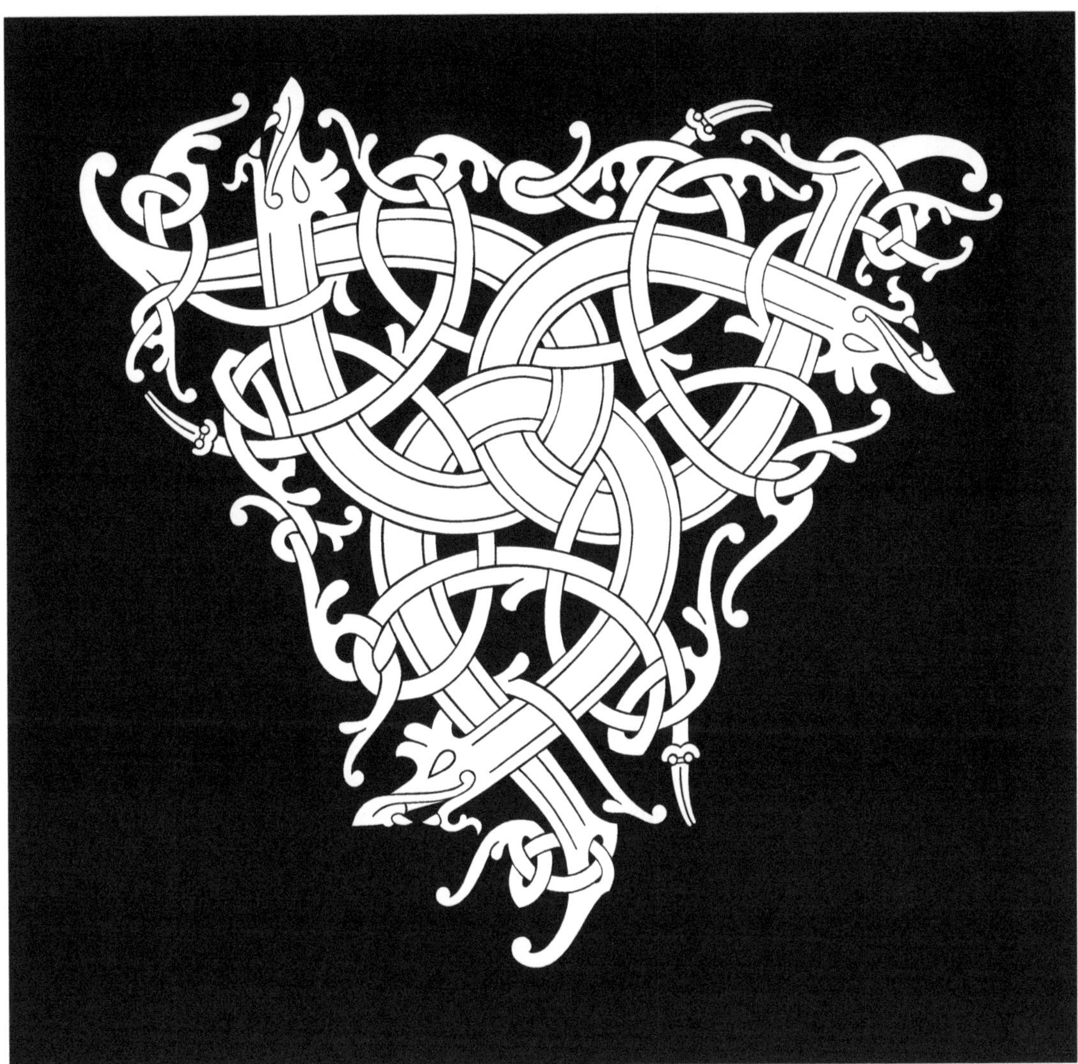

D

Motifs

- Great beast variations, typically a combination of a large carnivore and one or more serpents intertwined in battle (A, C, D).
- Mammals (A).
- Serpents (A, B, C, D).
- Birds (C).
- Masks (not displayed here, but very similar to the Mammen style masks).
- Vegetal ornaments (B).
- Rosette-like crosses (B).

Rise and Fall of the Great Norse Kingdom

The Conquest of England

King Æthelred the Unready paid the third Danegeld to Sweyn Forkbeard. But, owing to rumours of an assassination attempt against him, Æthelred then slaughtered a large number of the Norse settlers in what has since been known as the St. Brice's Day massacre. In retaliation, Sweyn raided England three consecutive times, before he and his son Cnut the Great finally conquered the kingdom. However, this was a very short-lived victory for Sweyn, who died a few weeks after.

Expansion and Subjugation

After Sweyn's death, his youngest son, Harald II, became king of Denmark, Norway and Sweden. Cnut was proclaimed King of England, but was exiled to Denmark. He returned the following year with a fleet, and regained control over England by defeating Æthelred's son, Edmund Ironside, in the Battle of Assandun. A few years later, when his brother Harald II died, Cnut seized control over Denmark, Norway and Sweden. The Scottish king also submitted to him, and Cnut was now king of the largest Norse empire ever, earning him the title, Cnut the Great. While Cnut was occupied in England, Olof Haraldson tried to seize the throne of Norway, but his attempt was futile, and he was ultimately killed in the Battle of Stiklestad.

Division of the Kingdom

When Cnut eventually died, his empire was divided into smaller kingdoms. Magnus the Good, son of Olof Haraldson, and therefore a legitimate heir to the Norwegian crown, although exiled to Novgorod, was placed on the throne of Norway at the age of 11. Harold Harefoot, son of Cnut, inherited the throne of England, and Cnut's other son, Harthacnut, became king of Denmark. Harthacnut eventually seized control of England a few short years later, when his brother Harold died. But it was not long before he too succumbed, ultimately ending the Norse rule of England for good. After Harthacnut's death, Denmark was ruled by Norwegian King Magnus the Good for a few years.

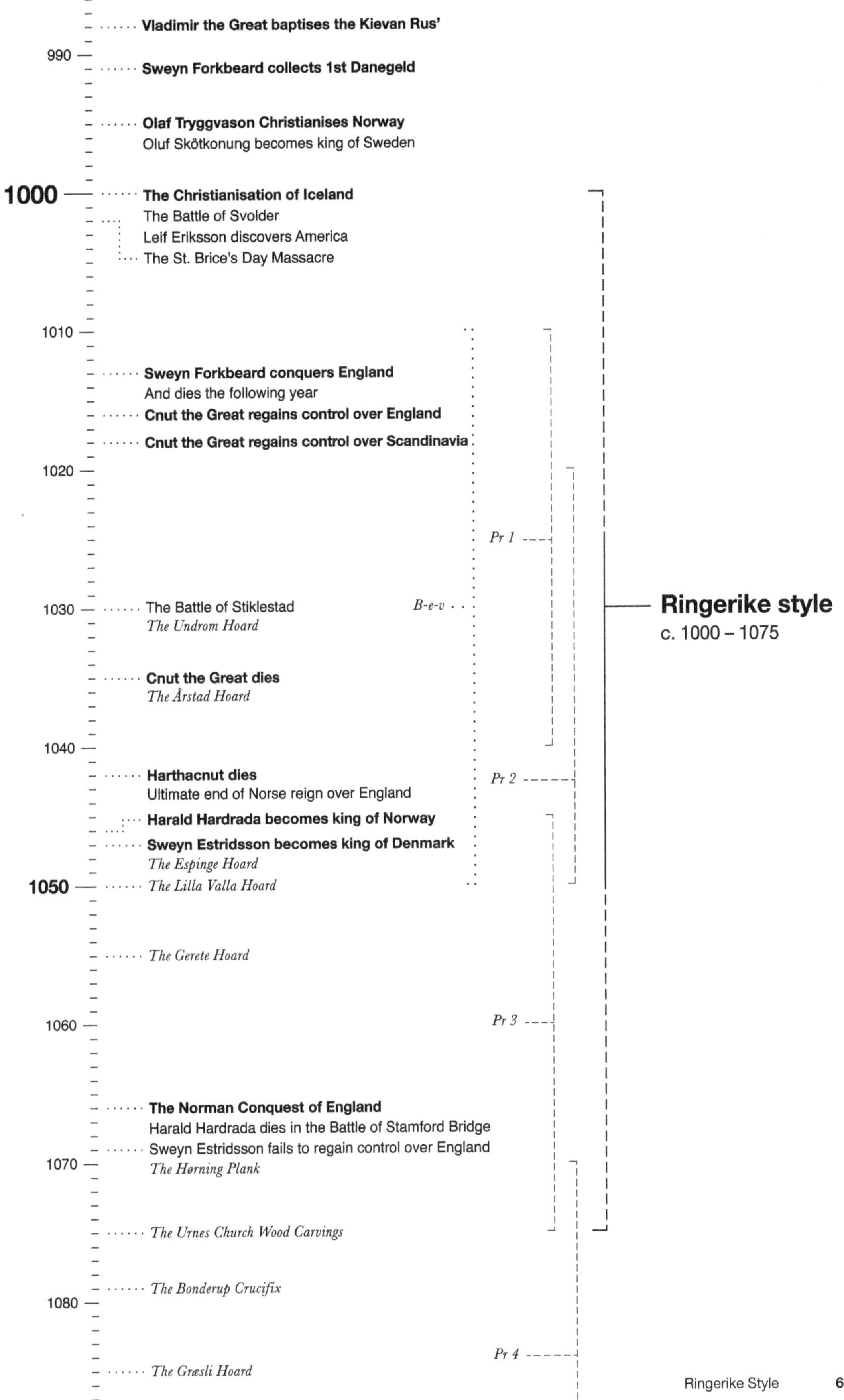

990
Vladimir the Great baptises the Kievan Rus'
Sweyn Forkbeard collects 1st Danegeld
Olaf Tryggvason Christianises Norway
Oluf Skötkonung becomes king of Sweden
1000
The Christianisation of Iceland
The Battle of Svolder
Leif Eriksson discovers America
The St. Brice's Day Massacre
1010
Sweyn Forkbeard conquers England
And dies the following year
Cnut the Great regains control over England
Cnut the Great regains control over Scandinavia
1020
Pr 1
1030
The Battle of Stiklestad
The Undrom Hoard
B-e-v
Cnut the Great dies
The Årstad Hoard
1040
Harthacnut dies
Ultimate end of Norse reign over England
Pr 2
Harald Hardrada becomes king of Norway
Sweyn Estridsson becomes king of Denmark
The Espinge Hoard
1050
The Lilla Valla Hoard
The Gerete Hoard
1060
Pr 3
The Norman Conquest of England
Harald Hardrada dies in the Battle of Stamford Bridge
Sweyn Estridsson fails to regain control over England
1070
The Hørning Plank
The Urnes Church Wood Carvings
The Bonderup Crucifix
1080
Pr 4
The Græsli Hoard
1090
Ringerike style
c. 1000 – 1075

A Blossoming of Foliate Ornaments

Development

The characteristics of the Ringerike style directly extend the Mammen style, from which it may often be difficult to differentiate. The development of this style draws further inspiration from Western European sources. The use of foliate motifs is intensified. The style displays intertwining tendrils inspired by Frankish conventions, alternating lobes and tendrils of British origin, and leaf-terminals inspired by acanthus leaves, which were popular in both the Frankish and British regions. But the style is still inherently Norse. All external influences were modelled to fit Scandinavian traditions and conventions, where the motif of the great beast introduced in the Mammen era increased in popularity, and many variations appear, particularly on the many new runestones erected at this time.

Dating

With the gradual introduction of Christianity to Scandinavia, goods no longer accompanied the dead to their graves. Therefore, dating relies almost exclusively on metalwork found in hoards that included coins, but may be reasonably well-established.

Runestones

Only a dozen stone sculptures had been erected in Scandinavia before the Greater Jelling Stone, except for the Gotland picture stones. The power centred around the Jelling dynasty was probably the driving factor behind the development of this style: with its connections to the Church, the direct cultural influences must have had an impact, also reflected in the style. The runestones, inspired by the Jelling stone, became quite popular, and it is from this time we see the most runestones erected in Scandinavia, with Uppland, Sweden being the innovative centre. The influence of English stone carvers is evident, and the craft may have been brought back to Scandinavia with the Norse settlers. The Ringerike style is the only Viking Age style that is not named after an actual find location. Instead, it is named after the area of Ringerike, a little north of Oslo, the source of the sandstone of which many of the runestones are made.

Weather Vanes

Some of the most magnificent examples of this style are three weathervanes from Norway and Sweden. Originally, they were metal standards or flags on ships' mastheads or prows, but survived because they were adapted and used as weathervanes on churches, and remained in use almost until modern time.

Wooden Staffs

The wooden staffs found in Lund and Dublin also deserve special mention here, because of their splendid animal-head terminals, reminiscent of the animal-head posts of the Oseberg grave.

Distribution

The Ringerike style was widespread throughout Scandinavia and all the Norse settlements, particularly in the British Isles, where it inspired many of the local styles, and even found great popularity in the Irish regions, were it was extensively adopted and, among other things, directly inspired a few manuscripts. It continued to be used in this region even after it faded and transitioned to the Urnes style in Scandinavia.

Examples

Dateable

c. 1018–1035
Disc brooch
– the Årstad Hoard
Årstad, Rogaland, Norway.

c. 1026–1030
Gilt silver arm-ring with animal-head terminal
- the Undrom Hoard
Undrom, Ångermanland, Sweden.
Historiska Museet, Stockholm SHM 1318

c. 1048
Silver brooch
– the Espinge Hoard
Espinge, Hurva, Skåne.
Historiska Museet, Stockholm SHM 6620:2

c. 1060–1079
The Bonderup Crucifix
Bonderup, Zealand, Denmark.
Nationalmuseet, Copenhagen 14190

c. 1055
Gilt silver disc brooch
– the Gerete Hoard
Gerete, Fardhem, Gotland, Sweden.
Historiska Museet, Stockholm

c. 1085
Gilt silver bird brooch
– the Gräsli Hoard
Gräsli, Sør-Tröndelag, Norway.
Trondheim Museum

Undateable

Animal-head staff (I)
Dublin, Ireland.
National Museum of Ireland, Dublin E172:5587

Animal-head staff (II)
Lund, Scania, Sweden.
Kulturen, Lund KM 59.126:795

The Alstad Stone
Alstad, Oppland, Norway.
Universitetets Oldsaksamling, Oslo.

Bone needle
London, England.
The British Museum, London M&LA 1893, 6–18, 72

Bronze rim mount
Aarhus, Jutland, Denmark.
Nationalmuseet, Copenhagen C9487

The Dynna Stone
Dynna, Oppland, Norway.

The Flatatunga Planks
Flatatunga, Northwestern Region, Iceland.
Þjóðminjasafn Íslands, Reykjavík 15296 a-c

Gilt silver bronze plate
Winchester, England.
Winchester Cathedral Library

Gold filigree disc brooches
– the Hornelund Hoard
Hornelund, Jutland, Denmark.
Nationalmuseet, Copenhagen C7144, C7145

The Gök Stone (Gökstenen)
Härad, Södermanland, Sweden.

The Heggen Vane
Heggen, Buskerud, Norway.
Universitetets Oldsakssamling, Oslo, C23602

Ivory head of a tau crozier
Veszprémvölgy, Hungary.

The Källunge Vane
Källunge, Gotland, Sverige.

The Norra Åsarp Stone
Norra Åsarp, Västergötland, Sweden.

The Gaulverjabær Plank
Gaulverjabær, Southern Region, Iceland.
Þjóðminjasafn Íslands, Reykjavík 1974:217

The Ramsundsberget Sigurd-carvings
Jäder, Södermanland, Sweden.

Stone from Allehelgons Kirke
Lund, Scania, Sweden.

Stone slab
City of London, England.

The Stora Ek Stone
Stora Ek, Västergötland, Sverige.

The St Paul's Churchyard Stone
St Paul's churchyard, London, England.
Museum of London, London 4075

The Söderala Vane
Söderala, Hälsingland, Sweden.
Historiska Museet, Stockholm SHM 16023

The Tullstorp Stone
Tullstorp, Scania, Sweden.

The Vang Stone
Vang, Oppland, Norway.

Urnes Style

c. 1050 — 1125

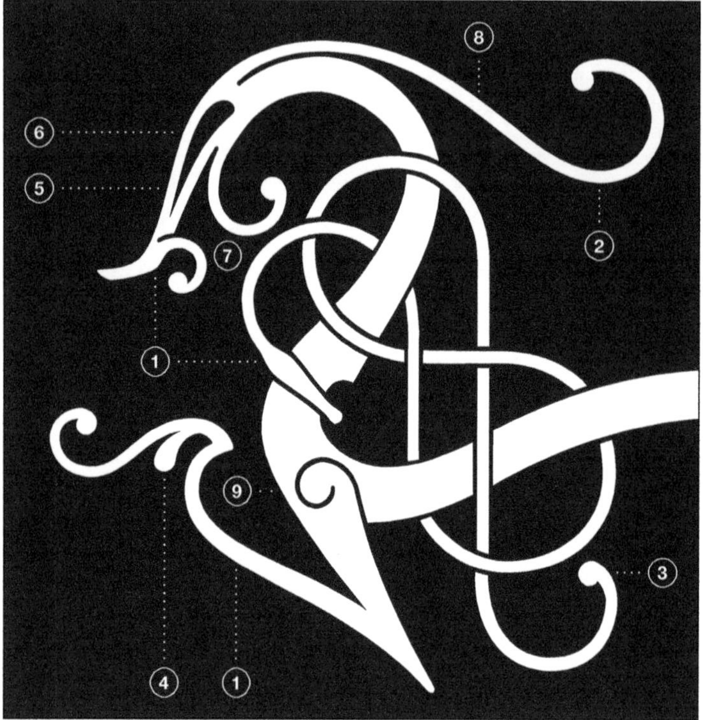

Shapes

1 Extremely elongated proportions (head reduced to almost a mere ribbon terminal).
2 Tendrils usually without offshoots.
3 Tightly scrolled tendril terminals.
4 Tendrils with a single lobe.
5 Head in profile.
6 Almond-shaped eye.
7 Upper and lower lip-lappets.
8 Neck tendril.
9 Spirals representing hip joints.

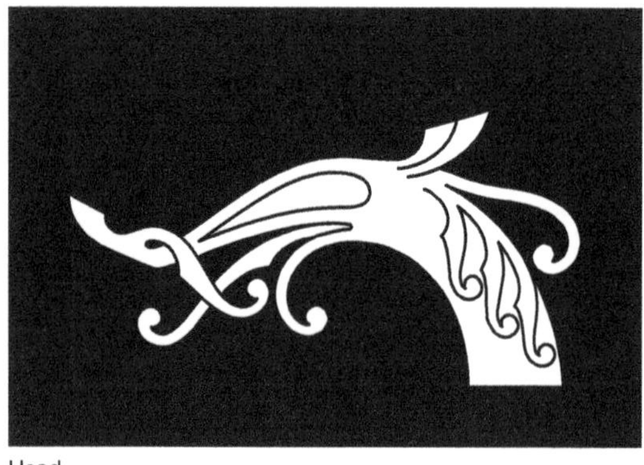

Head

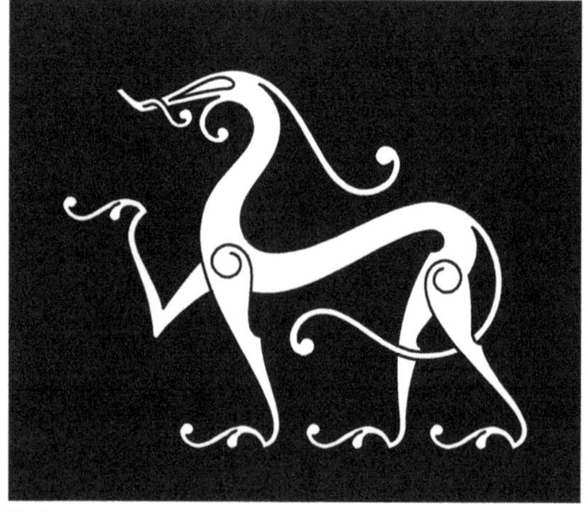

Body

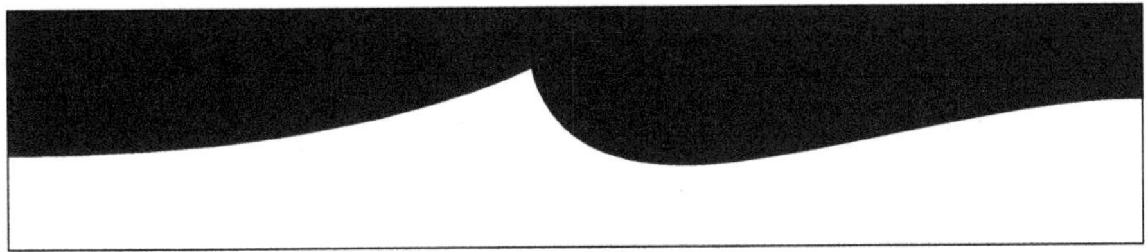

Outlines

Even outlines with slight tapering and almost without kinks and indents.

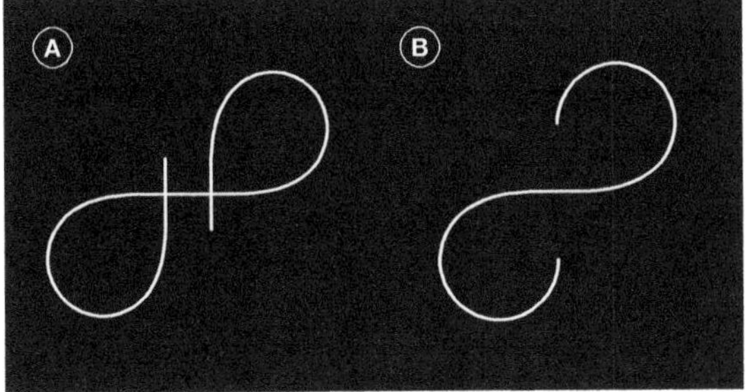

Flow

Circular curves looping in opposite directions

A Figure-of-eight loops.
B S-shapes.

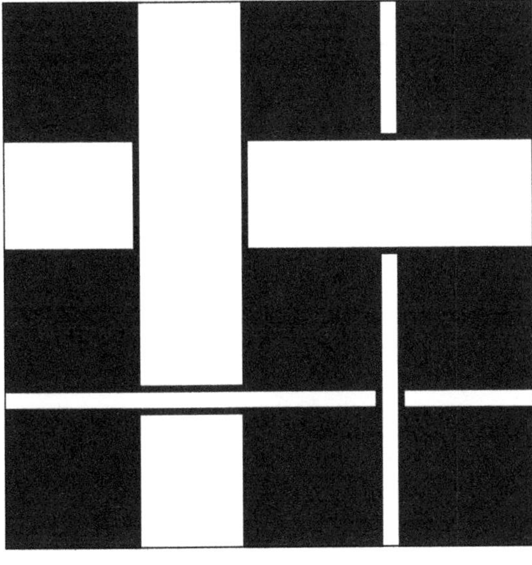

Pattern

- Open interlacing with a more visible background.
- Single-strand ribbons.
- Usually limited to only two ribbon widths.

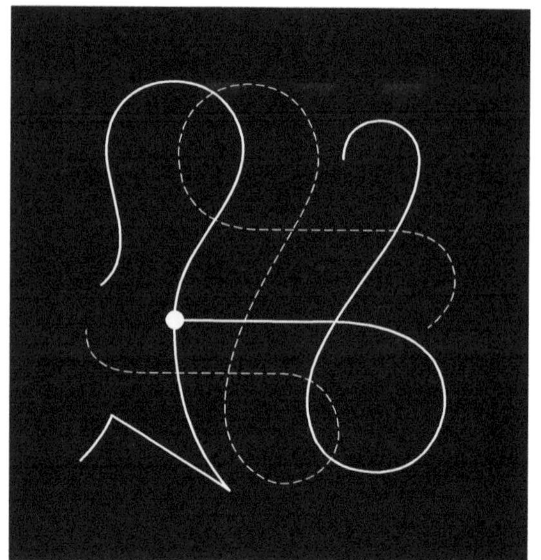
A

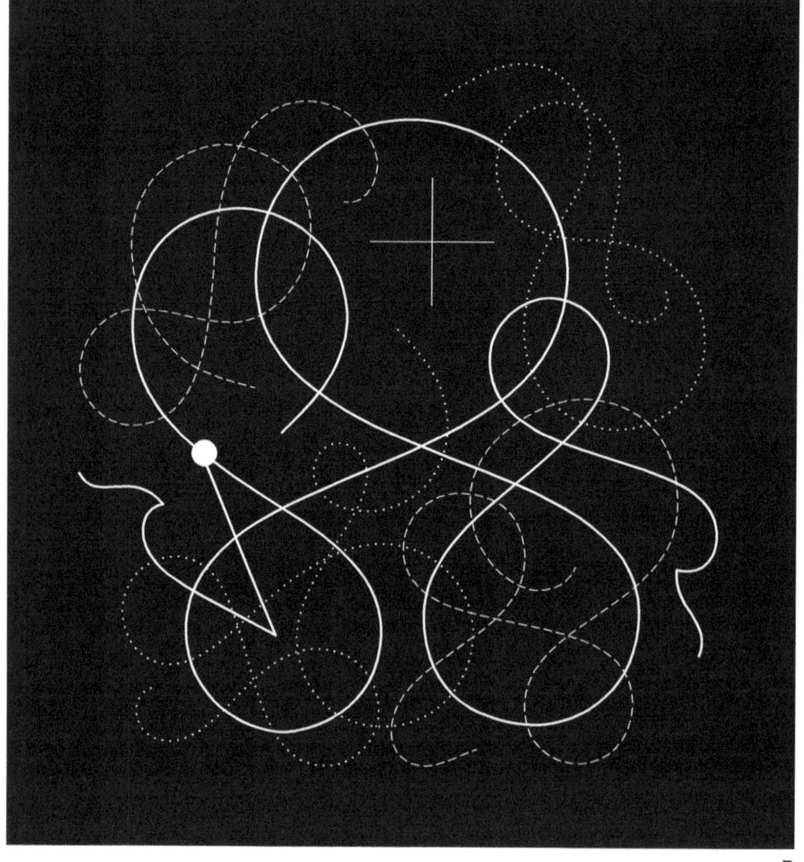
B

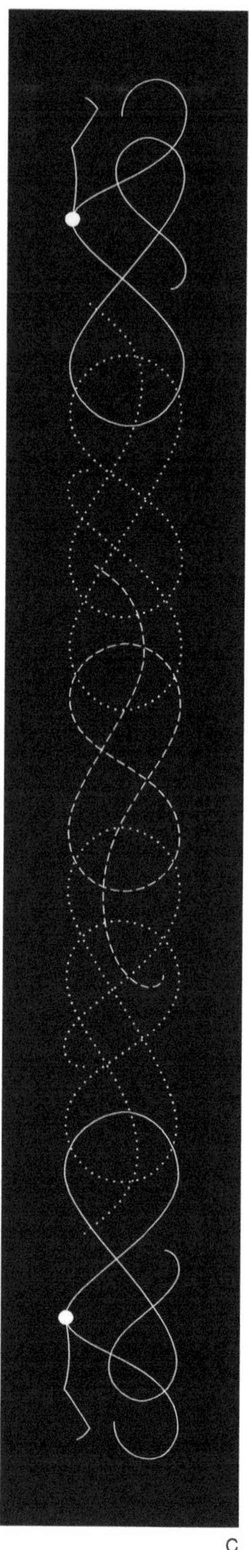
C

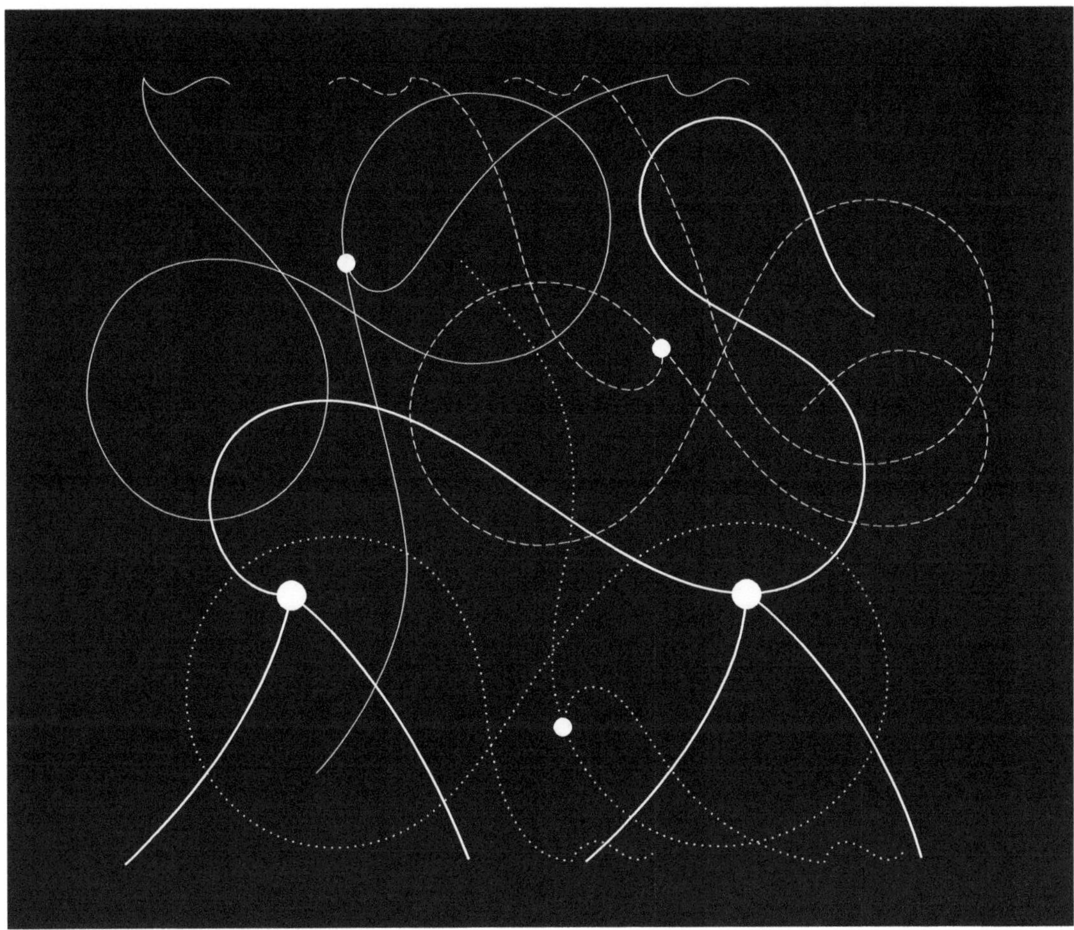

D

Composition

- Juxtaposed and interpenetrating ribbons of figure-of eight loops.
- Absence of axes and symmetry in composition.
- Balance in design is built by the fluid juxtaposition of the circular loops.

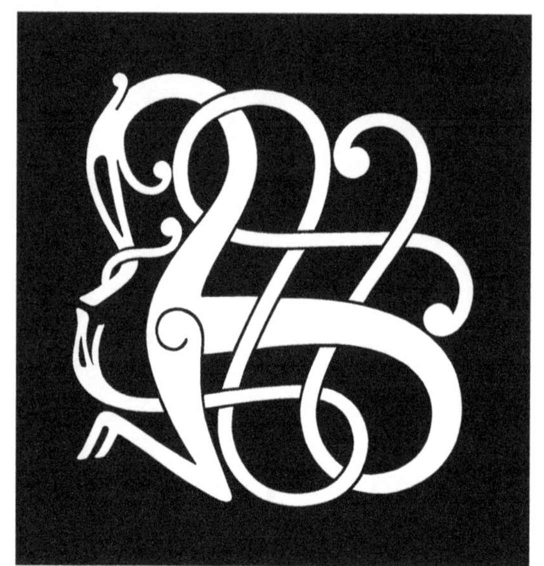

A

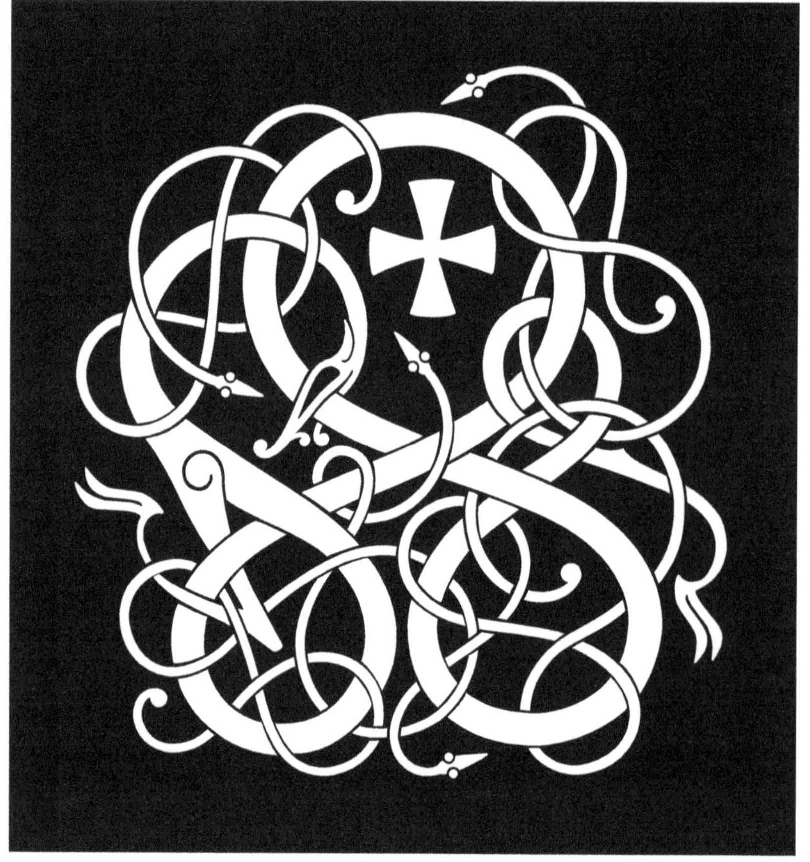

B

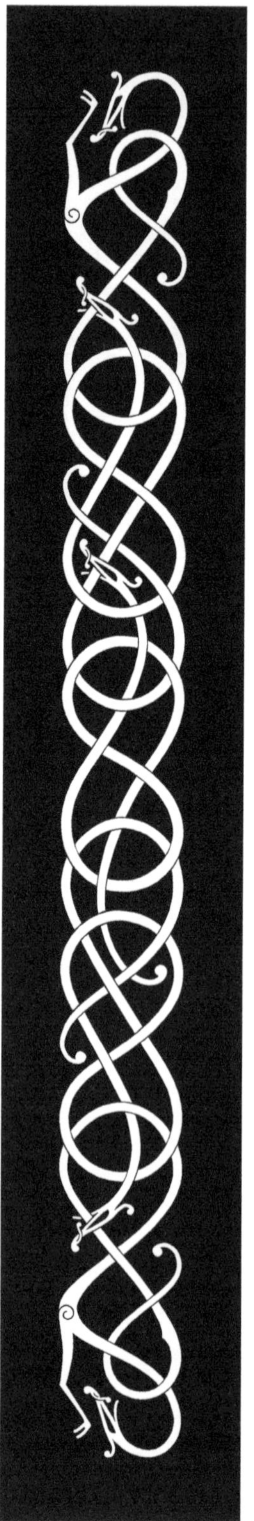

C

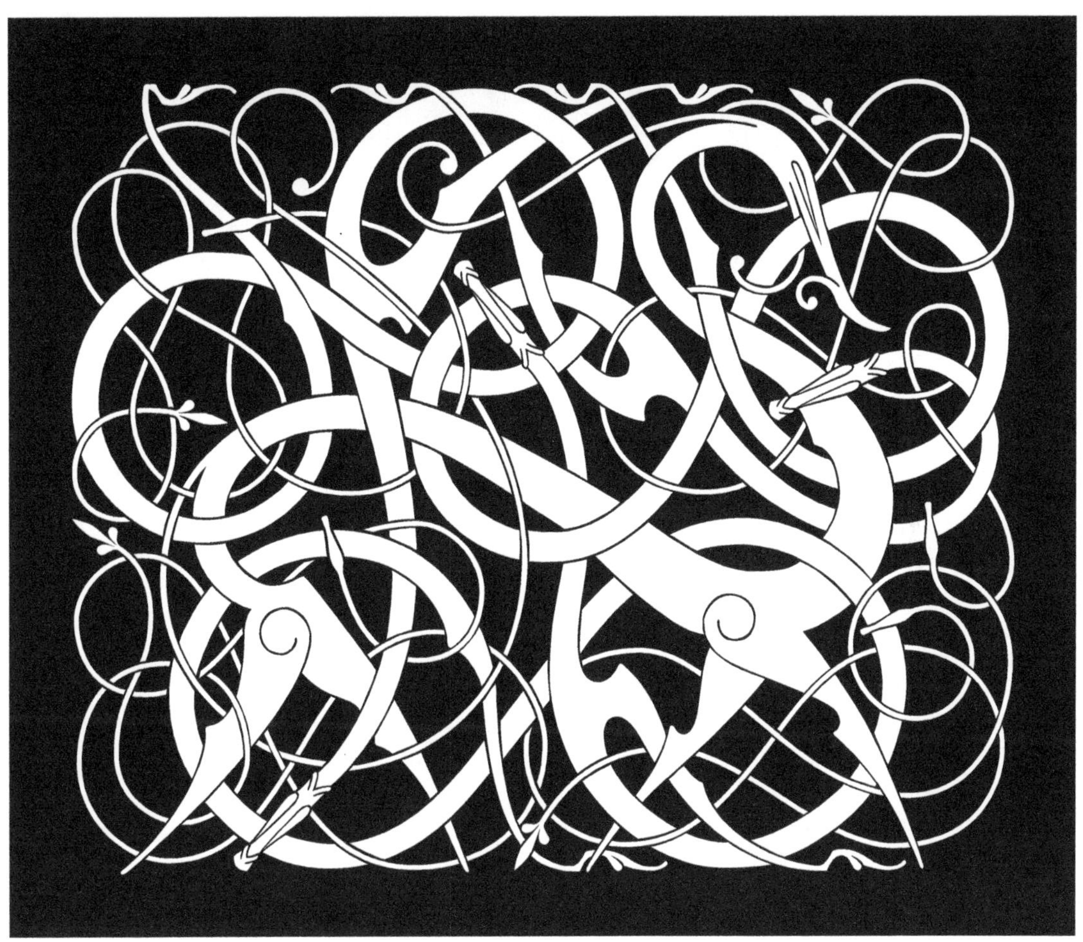

D

Motifs

- Great beast motifs almost exclusively, typically executed in a very similar and extremely formalised manner.
- Occasional vegetal motifs (not displayed here, although the terminals of feet and tails in illustration D have vegetal forms).

Consolidation of the Norse Regions

The Throne of Norway

Harald Hardrada, the half-brother of Olaf Haraldson, fled to Kievan Rus' after he and Olaf were defeated at the Battle of Stiklestad. He became a captain in the army of Yaroslav the Wise, king of the Rus', and later went to Constantinople, where he earned great honour and wealth serving in the Byzantine Varangian Guard. After fifteen years in the East, he returned to Norway just before the death of Magnus the Good, and soon became king of Norway.

The Throne of Denmark

Sweyn Estridsson, who had served under Magnus the Good, became king of Denmark. Though he was not a direct successor to Cnut, he was the closest living legitimate heir to the throne through his family connection to his mother, Cnut's sister, Estrid Svendsdatter, and he took the matronymic surname Estridsson, emphasising his connection to the royal Danish bloodline. Sweyn is often considered Denmark's last Viking Age king, as well as the first Medieval one.

The Norman Conquest of England

After securing his power as Duke of Normandy, William the Conqueror, who was a descendant of Rollo, launched the Norman Conquest of England and claimed the English throne. In his pursuit of the English crown, Harald Hardrada died in the Battle of Stamford Bridge, opposing the Anglo-Saxon king Harold Godwinson. Later that same year, Harold was defeated by William, who was then crowned king of England in London. A few years later Sweyn Estridsen made a couple of final attempts to reconquer the English throne to re-establish the Great Norse Kingdom, but failed. These events are traditionally considered to mark the end of the Viking Age.

The Conversion of Sweden

There were numerous attempts to convert the Swedish regions of Scandinavia, but they were not very successful, owing to the resistance of the Swedish people, with their deeply-rooted Norse beliefs and their strong traditions around the cult at Uppsala. None of the Christian Swedish kings had the strength or the support to force the conversion, until the reign of Inge the Elder, who was a devout Christian. He is known to have founded the first abbey in Sweden, and took harsh measures against 'heathen' practices.

European Integration

By now, all the Norse in Scandinavia and throughout Europe had converted to some form of Christianity. Their leaders grew dependent on the Church to support their rule, and at every level, the Scandinavian societies became increasingly similar in culture and customs to the rest of Continental Europe and the British Isles.

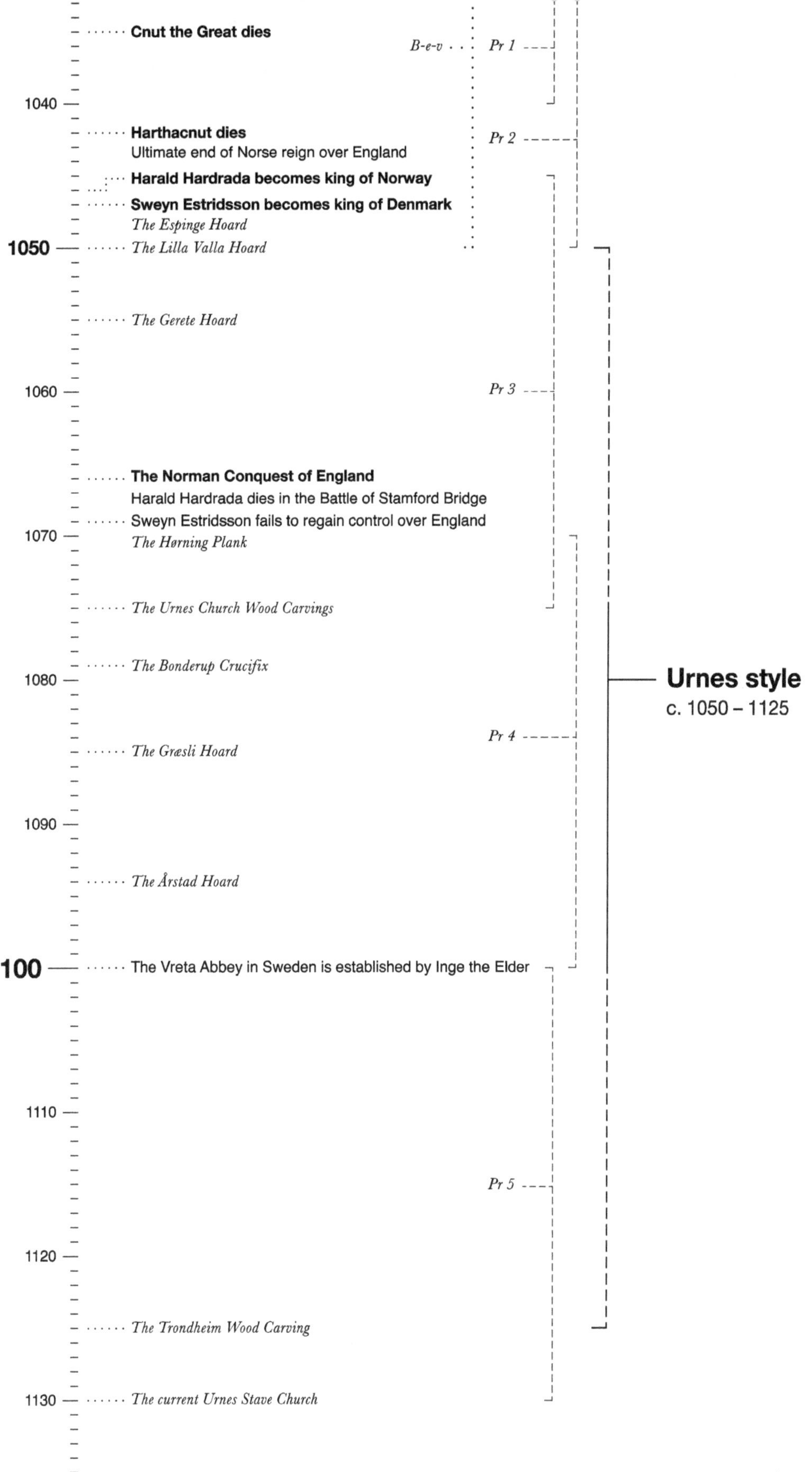
Cnut the Great dies
B-e-v
Pr 1
1040
Harthacnut dies
Ultimate end of Norse reign over England
Pr 2
Harald Hardrada becomes king of Norway
Sweyn Estridsson becomes king of Denmark
The Espinge Hoard
1050
The Lilla Valla Hoard
The Gerete Hoard
1060
Pr 3
The Norman Conquest of England
Harald Hardrada dies in the Battle of Stamford Bridge
Sweyn Estridsson fails to regain control over England
1070
The Hørning Plank
The Urnes Church Wood Carvings
The Bonderup Crucifix
1080
Urnes style
c. 1050 – 1125
Pr 4
The Græsli Hoard
1090
The Årstad Hoard
1100
The Vreta Abbey in Sweden is established by Inge the Elder
1110
Pr 5
1120
The Trondheim Wood Carving
1130
The current Urnes Stave Church
1140

Old Norse Minimalism

Development

Where the Ringerike style skews towards a greater elaborateness, with patterns that feature numerous tendrils and offshoots, the Urnes style is much cleaner, and almost geometric and modern. Though the two styles may seem very different in their approach to the execution of animal ornament, they share many common characteristics, including an affinity for the great beast motif originated in the Mammen style. On the other hand, in the Urnes style, plant-based motifs have vastly diminished importance, although they are not entirely abandoned.

Dating

The Urnes style may be approximately dated through dendrochronological samples of the surviving wood carvings, and dateable coins found in hoards with Urnes-style metalwork.

The Runestone Styles

The development from the Ringerike style may be traced through a large number of runestones that span the transitional period, and are found mostly in Uppland, Sweden. The runestone styles are categorised as 'Profile 1–5' (Pr 1–5) and 'Bird's-eye-view' (B-e-v). Pr 1, Pr 2 and the contemporary B-e-v pertain to the Ringerike style. Pr 3 is a transitional style that displays characteristics of both Ringerike and Urnes styles. Pr 4 is the Urnes style proper, and Pr 5 pertains to the late Urnes style.

The Jarlabanke Runestones

The runestones are virtually the only first-hand written sources authored by the Norse. They bear the names of those who raised the stones, as well as the names of those who the stones commemorate, and many of them were signed by the artists who created them, of which the runemasters Åsmund, Balle, Fot and Öpir are some of the best known. Through these runic texts, we get a tiny glimpse of the world view of the Norse. They describe events such as significant battles and the taking of Danegeld, also mentioned in sources outside of Scandinavia, and later medieval texts, such as the Icelandic sagas. From the inscriptions on a group of stones known as the Jarlabanke Runestones, we can piece together a reasonably cohesive picture of the family relations of the rich and influential Jarlabanke clan. The life of Estrid Sigfastdotter has been especially well-reconstructed based on the texts on runestones and other circumstantial evidence. She was the maternal grandmother of the chieftain Jarlabanke, a powerful woman born into the Swedish royal milieu, and one of the earliest known Christians in Sweden.

Openwork Brooches

A common Urnes-style find is the small openwork brooch featuring the great beast motif. The exact execution varies, but they all display a relatively simple figure-of-eight loop interlacing of a large animal fighting one or two smaller and thinner serpents.

The Urnes Stave Church

The magnificent wood carving of the Urnes Stave Church, from which the style takes its name, comes to mind when recalling great examples of this style. The carvings come from an earlier church built on the site, and were reused in the current surviving iteration of the stave church.

Distribution

The Urnes style is found throughout Scandinavia and the Norse settlements around Europe, and like the Ringerike style, it was partly adopted in Ireland and persisted there, even when its popularity had faded in contemporary Scandinavia.

Romanesque Art

In Norse regions, the Urnes style transitioned to, and blended with the contemporary Romanesque art, which dominated Christian European culture.

Examples

Dateable

c. 1050
Fluted silver bowl — the Lilla Valla Hoard
Lilla Valla, Gotland, Sweden.
Historiska Museet, Stockholm SHM 3099

(c. 1075)
The Urnes Church Wood Carvings
Urnes, Sogn og Fjordane, Norway.

c. 1070
The Hørning Beam
Hørning, Jutland, Denmark.
Nationalmuseet, Copenhagen D2309

c. 1100 – 1150
Wood carving from furniture
Trondheim, Trøndelag, Norway.
Vitenskabsmuseet Trondheim N30000/FH415

Runestone U 130
Nora, Uppland, Sweden.

Runestone U 177
Stav, Uppland, Sweden.

Runestone U 202
Vallentuna, Uppland, Sweden.

Runestone U 460
Skråmsta, Uppland, Sweden.

Runestone U 961
Vaksala, Uppland, Sweden.

Runestone Sö 276
Strängnäs, Södermanland, Sweden.

The head of a tau crozier
Thingvellir, Iceland.
Þjóðminjasafn Íslands, Reykjavík 15776

Undateable

The Ardre Stones
Ardre, Gotland, Sweden.

Bottom plate of 'box-shaped' brooch
Tjängdarve, Träkumla, Gotland, Sweden.
Historiska Museet, Stockholm.
SHM 3871

Box tomb in Vreta Monastery
Vreta, Östergötland, Sweden.

The Gåtebo Crucifix
Gåtebo, Öland, Sweden.
Historiska Museet, Stockholm SHM 100

Openwork bronze brooch
Östervarv, Östergötland, Sweden.
Historiska Museet, Stockholm.
SHM 9170:1216

Openwork silver brooch (I)
Lindholm Høje, Jutland, Denmark.
Nationalmuseet, Copenhagen ÅHM1937

Openwork silver brooch (II)
Tröllaskógur, Southern Region, Iceland.
Þjóðminjasafn Íslands, Reykjavík 6524

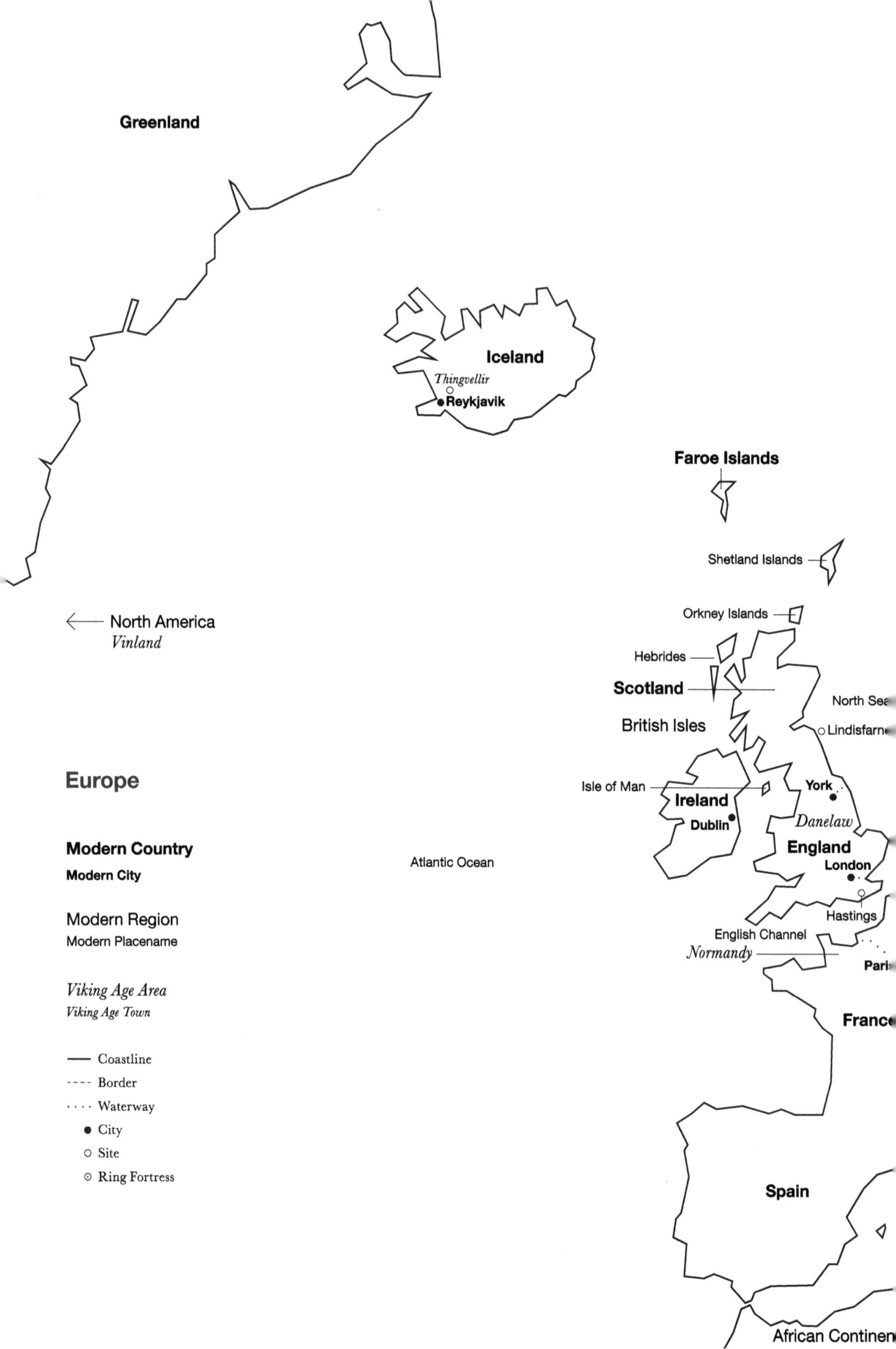

Greenland
Iceland
Thingvellir
Reykjavik
Faroe Islands
Shetland Islands
Orkney Islands
Hebrides
Scotland
North Sea
British Isles
Lindisfarne
North America
Vinland
Europe
Isle of Man
York
Ireland
Dublin
Danelaw
England
London
Modern Country
Modern City
Atlantic Ocean
Modern Region
Modern Placename
Hastings
English Channel
Normandy
Paris
Viking Age Area
Viking Age Town
France
Coastline
Border
Waterway
City
Site
Ring Fortress
Spain
African Continent

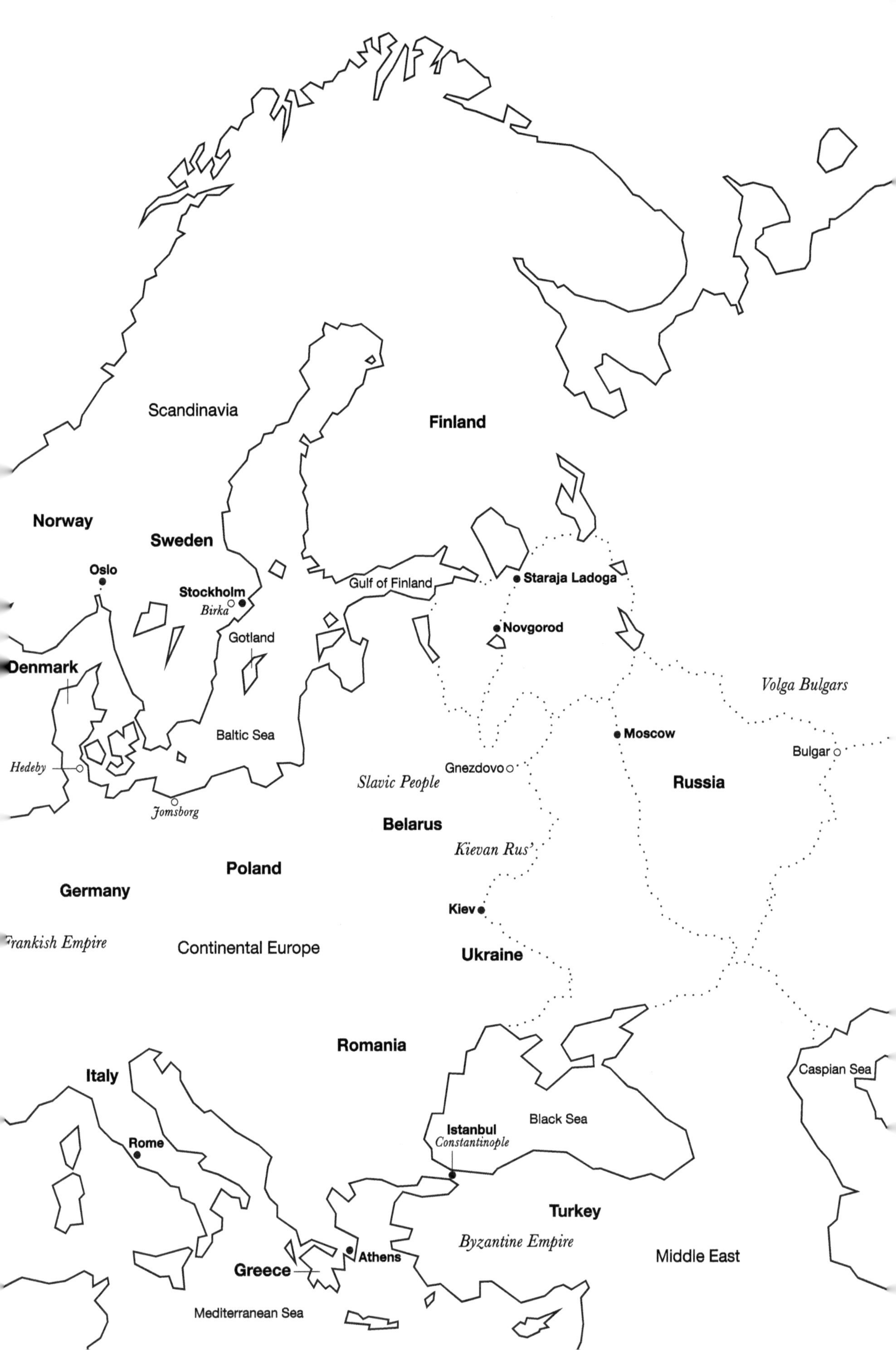

Scandinavia
Finland
Norway
Sweden
Oslo
Stockholm
Birka
Gulf of Finland
Staraja Ladoga
Novgorod
Gotland
Denmark
Volga Bulgars
Baltic Sea
Moscow
Hedeby
Bulgar
Gnezdovo
Slavic People
Russia
Jomsborg
Belarus
Kievan Rus'
Poland
Germany
Kiev
Frankish Empire
Continental Europe
Ukraine
Romania
Italy
Caspian Sea
Black Sea
Istanbul
Constantinople
Rome
Turkey
Byzantine Empire
Athens
Middle East
Greece
Mediterranean Sea

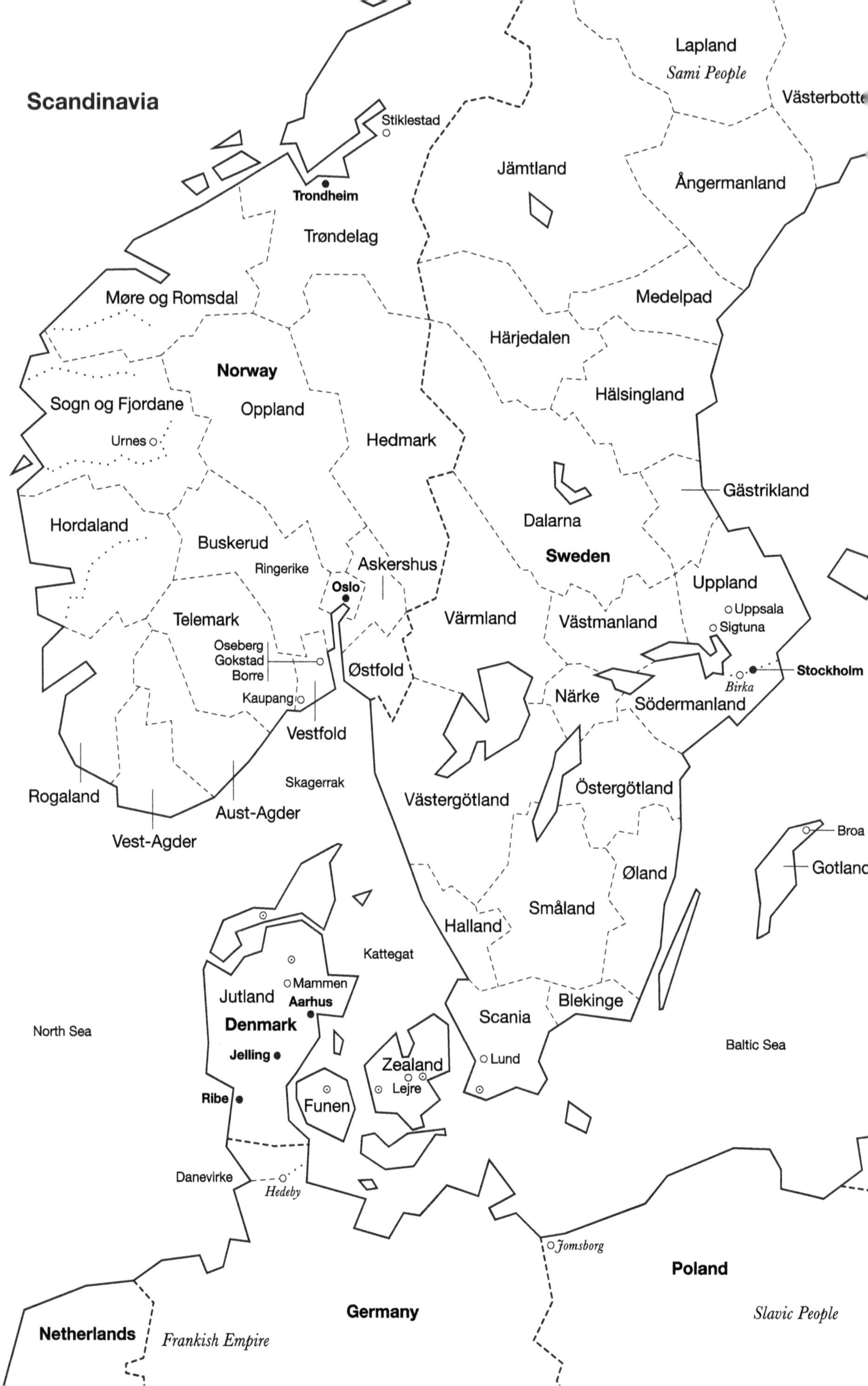

Scandinavia
Lapland
Sami People
Västerbotte
Stiklestad
Jämtland
Ångermanland
Trondheim
Trøndelag
Møre og Romsdal
Medelpad
Härjedalen
Norway
Oppland
Sogn og Fjordane
Hälsingland
Hedmark
Urnes
Gästrikland
Dalarna
Hordaland
Buskerud
Sweden
Ringerike
Askershus
Uppland
Oslo
Telemark
Värmland
Västmanland
Uppsala
Sigtuna
Oseberg
Gokstad
Borre
Østfold
Stockholm
Birka
Kaupang
Närke
Södermanland
Vestfold
Skagerrak
Östergötland
Rogaland
Västergötland
Aust-Agder
Broa
Vest-Agder
Gotland
Øland
Småland
Halland
Kattegat
Mammen
Jutland
Aarhus
Blekinge
Scania
Denmark
North Sea
Baltic Sea
Jelling
Zealand
Lund
Lejre
Ribe
Funen
Danevirke
Hedeby
Jomsborg
Poland
Germany
Slavic People
Netherlands
Frankish Empire

Resources

These are the resources I rely on the most in my work, and they have been crucial in researching and creating this guide.

Books and Articles

Signe Horn Fuglesang, 1982. *Early Viking Art.* Acta ad Archaeologiam et Artium Historiam Pertinentia (Series altera in 8°) 125–173.

Signe Horn Fuglesang, 1980. *Some Aspects of the Ringerike Style*. Odense.

Signe Horn Fuglesang, 1981. 'Stylistic Groups in Late Viking and Early Romanesque Art' *Acta ad Archaeologiam et Artium Historiam Pertinentia* (Series altera in 8°) I: 79–125.

James Graham-Campbell, 2013. *Viking Art*. London.

Anne-Sofie Gräslund, 2001. *Dating the Swedish Viking-Age rune stones on stylistic grounds.*

Asger Jorn, Bente Magnus and Gerard Franceschi, 2005. *Bird, Beast and Man in Nordic Iron Age Art.*

Asger Jorn, Bente Magnus and Gerard Franceschi, 2005. *Men, Gods and Masks in Nordic Iron Age Art.*

Jörn Stäecker, 2006. *Decoding Viking art, The Christian iconography of the Bamberg Shrine.*

Online Collections

The Danish Online Collection
samlinger.natmus.dk
flickr.com/nationalmuseet

The Norwegian Online Collection
unimus.no/foto

The Swedish Online Collection
mis.historiska.se
flickr.com/historiska

The British Online Collection
https://britishmuseum.org/research/collection_online/search.aspx
artsandculture.google.com/partner/the-british-museum

Thanks

I'd like to thank my patrons on Patreon for supporting my work and helping me spread the knowledge by making this guide possible.

With special thanks to

Mark Atchley
Paul Barker
Liaan Booysen
Tor Magne Bruun
Shane Curran
Arthur Von Eschen
Eric Grim
Doug Hull
Tim Hunter
Peter Lillian
Lene Lorentzen
Ashira Malka
Steve Nilsen
M. A. Poole
Gualter Reis
Eric Root
Olivia Tondevold
Nótt Úlfar
Jiří Vaněk

CPSIA information can be obtained
at www.ICGtesting.com
Printed in the USA
LVHW020454241020
669624LV00002B/12